Le Centre du Silence
Mime Work Book

LE CENTRE DU SILENCE

MIME WORK BOOK

By Samuel Avital

Forward by E.J. Gold
Author of "American Book of the Dead"

Wisdom Garden Books
Venice, California
1977

LIBRARY OF CONGRESS
CATALOGUE CARD NUMBER 77-84487
COPYRIGHT © 1975 By Samuel Avital
All Rights Reserved

PRINTED IN UNITED STATES OF AMERICA
First Edition Published by
Aleph-Beith Publishers 1975

THIS SECOND REVISED EDITION 1977 Published by
Wisdom Garden Books
Box 1241
Venice, California 90291

ISBN 0-914794-30-2

9, 8, 7, 6, 5, 4, 3, 2,

PRINTED by DELTA LITHOGRAPH CO. VAN NUYS, CA.

LE CENTRE DU SILENCE MANDALA

"There are so many of us now in motion, and like a child we are very curious, we ask, How long is the time? How great and far or near is the space. So many stars, like the hair on our heads that cannot be counted, trying to measure the timelessness and spacelessness. We starve to know, to apply, and become silent within, in these perplexed times we live now."

Samuel Avital

This book is dedicated in hommage and profound reverence to all my beloved teachers on all planes, who took what was offered, who gave what could not be taken. Toda Rabba.

Samuel Avital
Feb. 10, 1975

WORDS OF APPRECIATION FROM HEART TO HEART

I would like to thank the beautiful people, who collected, and typed the material here, without their help this would not be. Mainly ILANA GLASSMAN, CHRIS KANALY, LESLIE COLKET.

And also for their dedicated and untired work for the last few years in Le Centre Du Silence.

To my beloved friend MONI YAKIM, for his immense assistance and help for many years, and for his contribution to the book.

And to the dynamique PAUL CURTIS, the Director of the American Mime Theatre in New York City and the founder of the International Mimes and Pantomimists, and Administrator for its first year of existence (1974). Thank you, Paul, for being here.

And of course to my beloved teachers ETIENNE DECROUX, MARCEL MARCEAU, AND JEAN-LOUIS BARRAULT, who have instilled in me the knowledge and the love for this ancient-new art form, Le Centre Du Silence being their offspring, is surely at work.

For MAXIMILIEN DECROUX and his constant direction and guidance while I was in his Compagnie de Mime in Paris, for his focusing to the essence during the work. Thank you for this gift.

To TIM FULLER, who with his organic and contagious enthusiasm, wheeled the whole circle of love and creativity for the actualization and birth of this book.

And obviously for CARLO SUARES the illumined Kabbalist of our time, who with his insight and spiritual support for the inner reality, helped me realize why we are here.

And finally to my beloved grandfather ELIAHOU YAAKOV ABITBOL, who taught me about life-death through his teaching situations, silently and affectionately. May his soul rest in peace. Amen.

My beloved Grandfather, ELIAHOU YAACOV ABITBOL, Sage and spiritual guide of my young age, Kabbalist of the heart, and leader of his community, May his soul rest in Peace.

samuel avital

FORWARD

A thin, tiny sparrowlike man perches at the door, peering into the gloomy reddish glow of the room. He hesitates only a moment and then strides in.

Within the room he finds the elements of new space. Everything he once held secure he has dropped at the door, for he no longer needs them.

The man who dares — the wild explorer of equally wild spaces, is Samuel Avital — distinguished by no title, no diploma, no degree, no special honors, or awards of recognition — but only by the fact that he is genuinely, truly alive.

His great contribution is that others who have been touched by him, even though they were asleep and walking in the land of shadows, also become alive by virtue of his gift.

Is he a mime? Only if Solomon, Merlin and Gandalf were mimes. He does not move through space; he creates it as if solid and real.

He finds new uses for old things, and makes new things with new uses. The universe does not exist for him beyond the moment, and for those who walk with him, the universe becomes new, freshly made, and yet ancient beyond memory.

He forms mass, makes it appear in space, moves within and around it, stirs up realities that never were, until he thought of them; reflects absurdities that no one looked at until they appeared in his mirror of life; conjures people that no one has seen because they are the self . . . in short, he is master of the universe, yet can be claimed by no object within it. He knows, remembers, understands, feels, senses with all his heart. What more is there to say about a man?

E.J. Gold
June, 1977

Marcel Marceau on Samuel Avital

"Somewhere in Colorado, in a beautiful town called Denver, there is a community of young people directed by the very talented Samuel Avital. I think that his work is important, he brings awareness to the soul of people, and gives to the young dedicated artists who work under his direction the need, dedication and love for the world of silence, the beautiful Art of Pantomine."

Marcel Marceau, BIP.
Denver, November 20, 1971

Some were in Colorado, in
a beautiful town called Denver
there's a community of young
people directed by the very Talented
Samuel Avital, I think
that his work is importa
he brings awareness
to the soul of people,
and gives to the young
dedicated artists who
work under his direction
the need, dedication

And love for the
world of silence the
beautiful ART of Pantomime
Denver 20 Nov 71

Big

MARCel MARCeau

PUBLISHERS NOTE:

It is rare that a mime shares his art, his wisdom, his folly
with so many students. But Samuel Avital is more than a
mime, he is a mystic and must share. He founded the Boulder
Mime Theatre in 1971 and since then thousands have
attended Le Centre Du Silence Workshops. Originally the
Mime Workbook evolved out of those classes for his
students. Because of its popularity the Workbook found its
way into bookstores and into the hands of many who could
not attend. It has become an inspiration as a way to conduct
one's everyday life as well as a guide to students of mime.

If you wish to receive information about the work
of LE CENTRE DU SILENCE, please write to:

LE CENTRE DU SILENCE
Samuel Avital, Director
701 Arapahoe Ave., #206
Boulder, Colorado 80302

Table Of Contents

Introduction

A book on Mime? The art of silence. . . and with words? and from a Mime that deals beyond words? Absurd? Well, we Mimes see the absurdity as beautiful, and agree with contradiction.

According to my artistic experience, a Mime should, after a profound evolution in the work, give the proper importance to the letter, and explore the space between the words, like a Kabbalist who explores the space between the yes and no. Therefore, it is out of a need of growth of the teachings of LE CENTRE DU SILENCE, and its many increasing students who come here, that this is offered, and our way of exploring this work.

The popularity of Mime is growing today in America and the world at large, due to the life work of the 20th century great teachers of this art, Etienne Decroux, Jean-Louis Barrault, Marcel Marceau, Charlie Chaplin, and the work of the American Mime Theatre of Paul Curtis, the Pantomime Theatre of New York, of Moni Yakim, Claude Kipnis, Tony Montanaro and other devoted Mime workers, and the different schools of mime here and abroad, the influence of Mime upon film makers such as Fellini, the revival genius of Chaplin's films, and upon theatre workers of the new theatre, plus the spiritual awakening in this country, adds to that popularity among young people, who probably realize that words are often inadequate to express the essence of life, and being, and are not the only means of communication, of artistic self-expression, thus, they turn to that marvelous world of Mime, mother of all arts, to find their beautiful selves.

LE CENTRE DU SILENCE founded here in 1971, adds to this popularity and attracts those souls seeking to channel their energies through harmonious work on themselves here in our UNIQUE MIME WORKSPACE as we call it, and fulfill their needs, those who come in the future under the beautiful, and majestic mountains of Colorado.

Coming from a different background than American, I had to confront the knowledge of English, and mold it into my way of thinking, to communicate with my American students, not giving too much attention to the convential way of using English, speaking only when necessary, and expressing through images, gestures, body movement, which is the basic language of Mime. The goal is to express the thought as a whole in words, and keep it flowing like water, thus the way English is being used here, through these writings, trying to be as clear as possible.

The Material assembled here sums up in brief, some of the teachings and the experience of our few years of existence in Boulder, where the Mime Workspaces have been led by me, with the assistance of dedicated persons. Its purpose is to share with you that accumulated work done here, thus, it is a work book for the active students, as a guide, with no pretensions whatsoever.

Mime as it is taught here, as an art integrated in the deep roots of our being. It demands great discipline of self, and sincere dedication from those who come to the realization to explore and know the self through this ancient-new artform, the art of the void.

Throughout the texts there comes as a whole, a line or a non-line of our way of working, with its philosophical attitude, and its practicality of doing, the language used in our sessions, fusing and coming through words, images, pictures, and the rest.

To learn Mime properly, one has to go through changing the way of linear thinking. If you wish, Mime thinks movement, circles, mandalas, from a center. With exercise and attained experience, one can reach that multi-dimensional aspect of being, in order to illustrate, and communicate with it, and develop the artistic abilities, and awake the dormant talents within.

In our actual work we learn a topic or a subject by exploring every session through three phases.
1. The intellectual understanding of the subject.
2. The experience of it, actual working through definite exercises, knowing it through the body, and the psyche.
3. The application of it, the use of what was learned, an actualization of that specific work, individually and in group improvisation, or situation.

With the material learned properly in the session, the student practices daily, by my guidance, and with the investment of time, and effort, passing through other phases of the

craftsman to the artist, thus, gaining a genuine experience in this beautiful art, and use it in daily life.

Finally there is the BOULDER MIME THEATRE, also founded in 1972, and its purpose is to assist those who need to jump into the experimenting with that accumulated knowledge, with the alive audiences in the summer parks' community.

The apprentice student exposed, to share its learning, parading in the streets here, and in the actual performances, the audience stimulation, gives the opportunity to try out talents, changes and constructive criticism explored in depths, and in the harmony of being, one gains experience, and self satisfaction from the people's gatherings.

It is my hope, that this contribution will be of service to both those who have been active students here, and as a guide to those to come, our way, to embrace this work with us, and to every person interested in the arts, and ways people work together for the bettering of the SELF, in our times that mediocrity is king.

Some illuminating words here from Mimes at work in our times, will serve the student to meditate in its depths, and learn immensely from their insight.

My beloved teacher used to say, that the way you give is better than what you give, and it embraces wholly my spirit. The way this is offered is important to us, with the hope that the contained will become the container.

Thank you. And may Peace Profound be with you.

Evolution of Mime

Mime has similar origins to both drama and the dance. When the storyteller was at a loss for words, gesture took over. Because of its character as an instinctive part of the makeup of a human being, mime must, of course, have existed in some form as long as recognizable men and women have walked the earth. It must very early also have been a dramatic art used to entertain or interest the audience, just as early, in fact, as the tribal gatherings around the campfires of primitive peoples. We can be sure of this because of what we know of the brilliant mime and mimicry of many African tribes or of Australian aborigines.

When we get to Greece and Rome, we are on firmer ground. Aristotle in the Poetics writes forcefully about what he terms imitation. "Imitation is natural to man from childhood. . . and it is also natural for all to delight in works of imitation." From this is a short step to an audience delighting in a performance based on imitation—mimcry and its higher developments.

Dance and mime were then, as now greatly intermingled. The famous Phyrrhic dances of the Greek warriors, for instance, were partly a mimetic representation of different kinds of fighting. The importance of pantomime in Greek drama was underlined by the fact that the number of plays was severely limited, and therefore, much of the action had to be wordless.

In Rome the completely silent mime climbed to immense popularity. The legendary Livius Andronicus, having lost his voice, had the chorister speak the lines, while he mimed to the piping of the flute and the rhythmic clash of cymbals. Unfortunately, as was the case with the other arts, pantomime too was to decline. Its popularity was its undoing—it became increasingly vulgar and indecent in theme and action, as it pandered to the lowest public taste, and not unnaturally, as the Christian church became established, it fought against spectacles which were, more and more, reflecting and encouraging depravity.

Outside Europe, however, mime still flourished. Frequently, dance mime and drama had religious origins, as in India, and usually mime predated drama and then continued to exist as a parallel theatrical art. Dance drama (natya) in Indian goes back to that country's earliest civilization, when Hindu belief maintains that the god Brahma invented it, feeling that the ordinary man needed an art which would have no barriers of appreciation. Its first great teacher was the wise man Bharata Muni, so it became known, and is still known, as Bharatanatya.

There was mime too in China, which may well have the most ancient pantomime history in the world. A writer who lived in China in 100 B.C. tells us that there was a brilliant mime then called Meng, whose art was admired by one of the king's ministers. Chinese mime was beginning to develop into a tradition of total theatre, encompassing all the theatrical arts by the time of the early Middle Ages in Europe where the discredited players had taken once more to the roads and wandering life from which the Greek mimes had emerged. The minstrels and jongleurs of medieval times were the link with past glory, although they had music and storytelling skills, as well as mimetic ability.

As time went on, mime also found its place in dramatic history. It was a feature of the mystery, miracle and morality plays that developed in and after the twelfth century in France, Germany, England and elsewhere. During this time, the no drama, combining a gesture language with its sung and intoned text, became famous in Japan.

The static No theatre, which from the fourteenth century on used only three basic roles—the old man, the woman and the warrior—became a rather highbrow type of theatre, with the result that a more popularized form of the art began to develop, the kabuki.

Long before the seventeenth century, Europe had seen the start of a vitally important theatrical movement. Characters with some similarity to those of the ancient Roman mimes were appearing in a new form. Some authorities believe that the link between the Pappus, Maccus and Bucco of Roman days and the fifteenth-century Pantaloon, Clown and Punchinello is firm and complete. Along with these possible descendants came another—Arlechino (or Harlequin), who is suppoed to be a memory of the god Mercury. Italian and Sicilian players were especially adept at this new type of mime play, which was called Commedia dell'arte all'improviso—a comedy improvised by professional actors. Its influence spread all through Europe.

The most famous of the Commedia dell'arte characters are Harlequin, Pierrot and Columbine. When the commedia dell'arte spread to France, mime took on greater importance. The actors called forains, appearing at the great fairs, the Foire de Saint Germain or the Foire de Saint Laurent. They acted out of doors and at first scrolls covered with explanatory verse were shown as an accompaniment to the mimes. (This custom is remembered when Marcel Marceau's assistant shows us a card bearing the title of the coming scene.)

In the nineteenth century, two supreme and very diferent Pierrot-Clown protagonists emerged: Jean Gaspard Deburau in France and Joseph Grimaldi in England. Deburau became famous through the theatre des Funambules, was sought after by society, shouted for by his public, and eventually enshrined in history and legend. Deburau and his successors were subtle players, distilling understanding and sensitive feeling into their often rather muted performances. Grimaldi, on the other hand, had to broaden the technique to be successful. By his individual personality he became the forerunner of the modern clown tradition in theatre and circus, so much so that clowns are sometimes termed as Joeys in memory of him.

What has happened to Mime in the twentieth century? although the vogue for Pierrot and the mime plays had died down in Paris after World War I, the art of mime still fascinated theatre people. From time to time various theatrical

directors of genius included mime training for their actors. One of these is the illustre Jacques Copeau. One of his students was Etienne Decroux, who admired the idea of pure mime and is considered today to be the great teacher and theoretician of this art, who still has his school in Paris.

In Copeau's theatre there was also Jean-Louis Barrault, remembered mainly today by the film of Carne — Les Enfants du Paradis, and at one time was the director of the Odeon in Paris; and evidently Marcel Marceau who actually worked with both Decroux and Barrault, and is the living genius of mime, and legendary in his life time. Through his work, the American audiences on T.V. and in theatre halls have become familiar with mime. Charlie Chaplin's genius revival of his work makes one wonder about this marvelous art, and Jacques Tati, Jacques Le Coq, and others.

What are the present trends in theatrical mime, and what kind of future can it have? There is Adam Darius who became inspired with Les Enfants du Paradis; in Poland The Wroclaw Pantomime Theatre, the Theatre on the Balustrade in Prague with Ladislav Fialka; The Theatre of the Deaf, who study acting, modern dance, and mime, some of them worked with Marceau, the influence of mime in the work of the Living Theatre and Grotowski's work, and some of the actors of the Open Theatre who studied mime under Moni Yakim in New York, the American Mime Theatre that has been very active in the last 23 years directed by Paul Curtis, The Celebration Mime Theatre of Tony Montanaro, Claude Kipnis and others.

And of course the International Mime Festival held in summer 1974 in America, in Viterbo College, La Crosse, Wisconsin that presented some of the actual mime workers of today, such as Dimitri from Switzerland, Mamako Youneyama of Japan, Geoffrey Buckley of England, Antonin Hodek, USA, Robert Shields and Lorene Yarnell and Memagerie Mime of San Francisco, Yass Hakoshima, and Samuel Avital who is a direct link to the great mime teachers of the 20th century, and who embodies in his work the spriitual aspect of the creative artist, in his Le Centre du Silence in Boulder, Colorado.

The Unique Art of Pantomime

"In the age of noise we live in, it is sometimes wise to listen to what silence has to tell us."

—Avital

It is no paradox that in a world full of noise, of commercial and inane advertising, the silence calls to us. Man, the artist, deeply concerned with his art, searches out the original spiritual source in order that he may dream and meditate, rediscover his Self, and give of himself in action and in contemplation to the art of silence. And silence is the true being of mime and the philosophy of using the speech energy only when it is necessary. It certainly seems to me that we communicate better in silence and movement than in words.

In the evolution of civilization, the essence of the human being has been hidden from immediate awareness. This basic fact has caused an attribution of the artistic sense to visions of the reaches of "other worlds," when in truth the reality of every human being is Artist. This cannot be more simply exemplified than with the silent technique of Pantomime—the music of the soul.

The history of this nonverbal art goes back to times of primitive man. Having developed no spoken language as yet, the people of that time communicated through body movement, but the

origin of pantomime as the theatrical form we now know has been lost in the past with the ancients who created it.

Since then, the art of mime has passed through various periods of glory and obscurity, now coming into a dynamic age of classical and contemporary forms. It is being heralded by some artists as a means of mind/body harmonization, an expansion of the centering of consciousness. More famous among actual perpetrators are Charlie Chaplin and Marcel Marceau, masters in the illumination of this art form.

It is known, by practice and self-knowledge, that any art form has sprung up from a spiritual reality. Too many artists today have gone away from that spiritual reality, attaching themselves to only commercial and material aspects of art. They have to find the way back to that spiritual source and its processes, and remember that any art form originates from the depths of silence, the self-search for cosmic expression of the essence of life, which is in all. Then the artists' contribution will open new spaces in our consciousness.

The Work of Decroux

To begin a short review of the art of mime, we shall look first to the work of the man, Etienne Decroux. Practically every contemporary mime has studied under this French master, who, through his analytical study of the human body and its movements, has created or rediscovered his own special technique of work, a kind of ABC of practice, which he has been teaching since 1931.

An actor in the theater and films from 1923 to 1945, Decroux has interpreted a large array of characters from the works of Aristophanes, Shakespeare, Ben Jonson, Moliere, Tolstoi, Pirandello, and so on. He has directed and worked with the well-known film artists, Copeau, Gaston Baty, Louis Jouvet, Artaud, and Charles Dullin in Paris.

A brilliant actor and a born orator, Decroux entered the theater of Jacques Copeau to learn diction; later he became the apostle of silence, theoretician, psychologist, and master of mime. He worked with Jean-Louis Barrault long before the film, Les Enfants du Paradis, and had also as a pupil the well-known and well-loved Marcel Marceau.

Although Decroux studied with Copeau, it was not there that he developed his system of pure mime. From 1921 to 1928, he sought out the various aspects of mime that could be taught and followed through by the actor. His new school took into account the costume, properties, and best means of expression both in body and gesture. His creation of a new alphabet, the "ABC of mime," was hailed with enthusiasm. The comedian, who had previously been only a kind of glorified marionette, came now close to realism, and not only was a new style being evolved—it was a new art.

The pure mime is no longer a simple actor of pantomime using symbolic and comic gestures to achieve his part; he now partakes of the "Art of Silence." Decroux has said, "Ideas are incorporated in the mime work itself—otherwise, it would just be pantomime."

Decroux took into consideration all possible body movements—action, speed, and intensity in time and space—and defined clearly whether they expressed rational or abstract ideas. "All are geometrically calculated. Mechanical movement must become natural," he has said. Analytical cubism and ideal presentation of the form seem to have the greatest influence in his teaching of the heritage of the old mimes. Decroux is a great admirer of Rodin.

You can tell who a person is by their mouth.

Thus, he established a foundation of articulate and distinct movement. He localized the action, one step at a time, une chose a la fois, only one limb at a time in motion; "The mime takes a step to begin something—not to come back to it later and re-do it." It is only through complete attention to the extent of fulfillment of the action that one attains its real beauty. "The mime condenses space and time to the essence of it, he can represent the universe in the small space of a few square feet."

The actor may express everything with his body only. He can do this without words, costume, properties, disguise, even without facial mimcry, as all these all too often demonstrate how small, mediocre, talkative, and inexact a scene can be. The mime seeks to develop an art, an art which is a contrast to that of the dance. "Dance is ethereal, Mime is solidly rooted in earth," says Decroux. "Whereas dance with music throws off bodily bonds, the mime in comparison seems static and silent."

Decroux made a great case of exactitude and clarity in form and became a doctrinaire and severe formalist. He created a repertory—Mime Statuaire, or Mime Subjectif—a repertory of expressions of the human form. Fundamental examples of these are "The Sporting Man" and "The Man of the Salon," the former having a body bent forward and curved; the latter, straightly erect.

Second and principally, Decroux made

pertinent and vital what he calls the Mime Subjectif; that is to say, with the techniques of exact suggestive reactions and imagination, one "sees" an object that is not actually there. This seeing replaces the object itself. The Mime therefore will fully evoke the concrete object through simple movements and gestures.

Jean-Louis Barrault

Then came Jean-Louis Barrault, the unorthodox pupil of Decroux, who asks the questions: "How can we express the silence, the solitude which is alive inside of us all the time?" "How can we recreate outwardly for all to see the intimate life which is lived in secret?" Mime, or the art of life which endures, makes endurable to the greatest possible extent the life we live—this art comes from a tragic or dramatic situation.

In his book, Reflexion sur le Theatre (1949), Barrault recalls that at the Decroux school nothing more than walking in place (a mime technique that gives the illusion of real walking) was practiced for three months in order to perfect this particular technique. As in any field of endeavor, the simplest things are always the most difficult things to accomplish. To walk in control, one must understand that it involves being on the balls of the feet with the back straight, chest forward, head erect.

The first "must" for the student of mime is the control of the spine, vertebra by vertebra. All gestures, all body positions—the arms, legs,

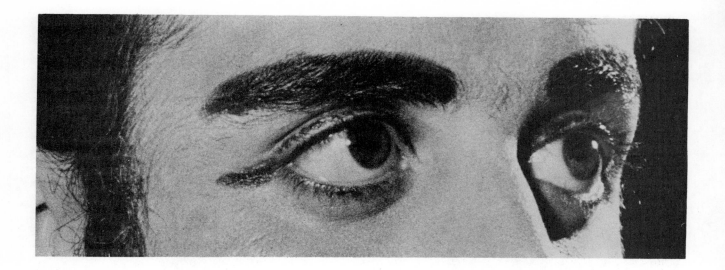

chest, and head—are regulated through the positioning of the spine. This represents the fundamental basis for the individual mime's style.

Barrault's first triumph as a mime was "The Horseback Rider," which later became such a marvel of grace and imagination in mime that it has become legendary. He received acclaim for the film, Les Enfants du Paradis. A special ballet-pantomime was adapted for this film by Jacques Prevert, which Barrault performed with Etienne Decroux and which he later incorporated in the repertory of his theater. Today Barrault is a speaking actor.

Marcel Marceau

This great mime genius studied in 1944 with Dullin and Decroux for two years—a relatively short period of training, in which he made himself known. "Mime is the drama of the human being in his most secret aspiration," Marceau says. "In identifying ourselves with the elements that surround us, the art of mime makes visible the invisible, makes concrete the abstract."

Marceau is incontestably the most noted mime of our day. In relying on all he had learned from Decroux about the old techniques of the Great Debureau, he nevertheless created his own personal blend of pantomime and mime which included as well some elements of the clown and the music hall. His style exercises present the grammar of the Decroux school in simple examples such as walking place, walking against the wind, pulling fishing lines, and so on. Alone, Marceau accomplished a seeming miracle: a single person on stage, without props, without special lights, without music, but who, through a series of simple changes of gestures, succeeded in filling the stage space with characters—a performance of solo interpreter that kept the audience on the edge of their seats.

One of Marceau's most poignant studies, "Childhood, youth, old age, death," while obviously derived from the work of Barrault, bears nevertheless Marceau's own stamp—his "Poetic Halo," as it has been called. This Halo is gesture which must inspire and reveal. The mime actor must vibrate with gesture as do the strings of a harp. He must be lyrical or almost musical, and thus transforms mere gestures into a bodily movement. Even in standing still, there must be fluidity.

At the peak of his career, Marceau seems to perform alone in his work; yet in the beginning his work was aimed at ensemble mime. "There are times on stage when one cannot make all expositions oneself," Marceau declared in a conversation with Herbert Ibering in 1956. "Alone, I would never have been able to mime the story of 'The Cloak.' Alone one can only express a certain person in a particular element; for example, a man climbs a stairway, then becomes the stairway; Bip (the personage creation of Marceau), playing the role of the lion tamer, gradually reveals himself as the lion; he catches a butterfly, and the simple movement of his hands becomes the butterfly—these situations are clearly seen by the public when the mime is alone on the stage.

Conclusion

After this brief presentation of the work of these masters of the art of mime, we must know, then, that actually there are very few who practice it, which is understandable because of the long, hard training that one must go through, and the strenuous exercises one must practice in order to develop a fit body.

In my experience and practice, it is indeed so. The techniques of mime can help one integrate one's mind and body. Harmony of the mind develops through using one's imagination and becoming aware of the movements, actions, and reactions one has used in presenting oneself. When the muscles and breathing are truly moving in tune with the mind, the psyche is free to experience the meanings of subject and object, time, space, and consciousness.

It is said that the art of mime is outside or rather beyond all instinct. To develop it, one must continuously work on supple and strong exercises of both body and mind. The mind must be constantly awake and aware; one needs to develop a strong will without defiance or weakness, and the student of mime must have an ideal within his heart. Only through complete attention to the exact fulfillment of the action can one attain its true beauty. The mime must be able to miniaturize space and time; he condenses an eternity in gesture.

Because silence is the foundation of mime, the artist is challenged to invent new ways to symbolize and communicate ancient truths. For this reason, this art centers around universal situations. When a mime treats war, he does not say which war; it is war, transcending boundaries of languages and countries. The mime uses no texts, no sound, and no set, for the only text is the actor himself and the audience is the set. The mime thus creates a total, relevant experience akin to the ritualistic and religious origins of theater, and the time, before the actor and audience become separated by invisible, psychological barriers.

Therefore, self-awareness is the key word and the core of this work. It is not a simple matter to gain control over the body "so that the elbow will listen to you"; it takes work but I am confident that anyone who wishes can learn.

All this can be achieved by that attunement to the spiritual reality we mentioned before. Until the so-called artist is in touch with that source to discover his ultimate creativity in himself, we are not going to see or experience any light in the arts. In mime, the performer, the performed, and the performance have to be embodied in one person; thus, it is necessary to train oneself to tune to the vibrations of the audience and, with the silence—the helper on the way—achieve that unity among all present.

In fact, it is meditation in action—a performer, an audience, and silence—all in the same space, sitting quietly and SEEING the reflections of themselves. It is as if the thought has taken form, and with the image that speaks there is communication. However, it is known that words do not describe the essence; they are symbols to reality. The mime has the ability to embody that essence and let it shine through motion in silent space and express it clearly.

For me, mime is more than an art, however; it is a way of life; it requires metaphysical as well as physical awareness. It is an extension of the life force for channeling the energies; it is a symphony of being.

In the age of noise we live in, it is sometimes wise to listen to what silence has to tell us. Rhythmic inner music, which is in us at all times, is only to be discovered in order to know ourselves and to live better. This after all is the purpose of art.

American Mime

An Interview with Paul J. Curtis

Paul J. Curtis—Founder/Director of the American Mime Theatre, Chairman of American Mime, Inc., and Founder of International Mimes and Pantomimists. Mr. Curtis has taught, lectured, directed, and performed since 1952 and has created a unique performing art—a complete theatre medium called American Mime. The history of American Mime is fully documented and available to the public at the Research Library of The Performing Arts, Lincoln Center, and Harvard College Library, Theatre Collection.

I asked Paul Curtis to comment on the American Mime medium for this book and the interview he sent me seems to emphasize and embrace our spirit at work in Le Centre Du Silence in Boulder. This interview is copyrighted by Paul J. Curtis 1975.

Q. Where were you trained and what motivated your departure from traditional Mime?

PJC. I was trained by Erwin Piscator at the Dramatic Workshop of the New School of Social Research. Following this training, I went to Europe to explore different forms of theatre. I was disturbed by what seemed to me the arbitrary separation between the arts of acting and dance. For example, from India to China there are no separate words in any language for dancer and actor. While in Europe, I discovered such things as the Peking Opera, and the work of French pantomimists, among other forms. I was struck by the silence of the French Mime, although I felt their product was innocent of the discoveries of the modern dance and Stanislavsky's contribution to the art of acting. Returning to this country, I thought it would be interesting to present for American actors a project of Mime that would at once demonstrate its potential and correct the limitations of the medium as practiced by the French. That project resulted in a concert at the 92nd Street "Y". This concert produced an unusually strong audience reaction to a product which was not overloaded with merit. However, the company, fortified by this audience reaction, wanted to continue and as a result The American Mime Theatre was created.

Q. What is Mime?

PJC. A definition of Mime is as impossible as a definition of acting or dance. It's like trying to tell you what water tastes like. Mime is a performing art that is defined by each performer and school that practices it. Because the art form lies between the two arts of acting and dance, any definition must reflect the acquired skills and ability to perform that which neither the actor or the dancer can do better.

Q. Is there a difference between Mime and Pantomime?

PJC. The word Mime embraces many diverse forms of the art. It is like the word dance which covers, with equal accuracy, an Ojibway tribal celebration, the classic ballet, or the tap dancing of Buck and Bubbles. The French School uses the two terms synonymously which has generated a great deal of confusion. In the American Mime Theatre, we use the following definitions because they are useful. Pantomime is the art of creating the illusion of reality by dealing with imaginary objects or situations. Its art rests on the ability to imply weight, texture, line, rhythm and force to the air around them. Mime, on the other hand, is the art of acting silently through various kinds of theatrical movement.

Q. What is the difference between American Mime and the French School of Mime?

PJC. The French School of the art is primarily that of Pantomime. Pantomime engenders in the viewer a feeling of credibility by the way the practitioner handles the air around him. We use very little Pantomime.

American Mime is a medium for silent actors who play symbolic activities in characterization and express the feelings and desires of their characters honestly through a kind of motivated movement we call form.

Q. You are credited with creating the Mime tradition called American Mime. How would you describe this work?

PJC. In the first place, I did not start out to create a new Mime tradition. I wanted to create a dramatic event that would combine acting and moving to produce a more meaningful theatrical experience. This work slowly produced a different performing art from that of the traditional French Pantomime. American Mime is simply a particular balance of the arts of acting, movement, Pantomime, design, and playwriting.

The two most important facts about American Mime are these: First, it is a complete theatre medium in a way that no other Mime form I know of is. That means there is a complete body of aesthetic laws and limitations governing every aspect of its activities from performance to script material that insures the consistency of its aesthetic products.

Second, The American Mime Theatre has functioned as a professional Mime company continuously for over 20 years making it the oldest professional Mime theatre in the world. This company was the first professional Mime company in the Twentieth Century in this country. It was formed in 1952 when there was no professional Mime activity in the United States and no European Mimes had performed here.

Q. What kind of material does The American Mime Theatre perform?

PJC. The primary aim of our medium, regarding script material, is to explore the internal landscape. We create mime plays that are made up of activity symbols. These activities must be logical on the narrative level and yet clearly communicate the symbolic significance behind them. Our content is myriad forms and facets of spirituality. It is our aim in performance to elicit from the audience through their intellects and emotions a direct spiritual response. While all of our plays are symbolic, some are more abstract than others. In most of our plays, the acting values dominate the experience. All American Mimes are trained to develop script material in our particular form of group creation. Our entire Repertory has been developed in this manner. We choose each play out of what individually and collectively concerns us most at the time of creation and in relationship to what we already have in the Repertory. In performance, from 5 to 7 different plays are performed, each of them representing a different aspect of American Mime script material.

Q. What theatrical equipment do you employ in your performances?

PJC. Our performers appear in black skintight units before a white cyclorama. Sets are never used. Masks, costume, properties, and set pieces are used sparingly and are created to be frankly theatrical. We try to produce a lean clean look by using equipment created to suggest more than it shows.

Someday you'll understand.

Q. Do you use music?

PJC. We use very little music. Our sound ranges from abstract vocal sounds made by the performers to electronic scores.

Q. Do the performers speak?

PJC. No, we don't. Although once in a great while the play will contain a special use of one word.

Q. Do you use white face?

PJC. No, we don't. That tradition began in the commedia dell'arte. It was originally the theatrical signature of a doltish character from upper Bergamo who was a baker's assistant and the white powder was simply the theatrical equation for flour on his face. The French school uses this device rather successfully as part of its mystique to accomplish a deft separation from the social experience. In a performance, our performers may play in 5 or 6 different mime plays, and the use of white face would seriously limit the possibilities of achieving the separation between characters and the dynamics of the plays.

Q. Describe the training program at the American Mime Theatre.

PJC. Our beginning course involves the process of the student becoming proficient in both acting and moving. The control and skill of the body must be fused with the motivation of the actor. To achieve this proficiency, we first must get, both individually and collectively, a psychological freedom that enables the actors to touch and use their truest responses in the performing process. We work on acting skills in the areas of motivation, characterization, objectives, and interplay, through our own form, which is the extension of our character's feelings into the body in accord with the dynamics of the particular play.

Q. What are the requirements to study at your school?

PJC. The only requirement is motivation. To begin, you must commit three months of unbroken study and work outside of class for ten minutes a day. While this demand may seem slight, it is beyond the capabilities of 99% of the non-professional students. Most students, while fond of the concept of themselves as performers, are totally unequipped with the motivation to seriously study any performing art. Or more simply, their innocence obscures the inherent price of progress—which is intense and continued effort.

Most students who study anything are not truly interested in achieving proficiency. They are there for other reasons. The student who achieves professional proficiency needs only one thing: motivation. This simply means that it is essential that the student understand that no one is responsible for their creative product but the student. When that is clearly understood, the student is introduced to the heady concept that any improvement achieved is produced by the accuracy and amount of work that the student does outside of the class structure. That concept generally takes two years to understand.

Q. Are there other Mime companies in the country?

PJC. Probably while you asked that question three others were formed. Mime activity in this country is growing so fast that we who practice it can barely keep abreast of its development. Every week there are new practitioners and new companies. We formed an organization called International Mimes & Pantomimists out of the need to keep all of us in the profession abreast of what's happening.

Q. Could one make a living as a professional Mime?

PJC. Probably not. After 20 years, we are just beginning to make a living. The most proficient practitioners of the art form have great difficulty in making a living; and until you achieve that same level of proficiency, which generally takes about six years, it would be highly unlikely. The American Mime Theatre has been funded by the New York State Council on the Arts, The Rockefeller Foundation and others, and we still have great difficulty in making ends meet. Mime is one of the last fields of endeavor one should enter to insure one of financial stability. On the other side of this, the opportunities for professional mimes today are expanding with a rapidity that would have seemed unbelievable even a few years ago.

Q. What is your reaction to the increasing popularity of Mime in the country?

PJC. I am both delighted and concerned. Delighted because for these art forms to take their place as equals beside the other performing arts we need many more practitioners, training schools, performance experience and justified critical acclaim. I am concerned with the growing number of people who, without credentials, call themselves mimes or pantomimists, who are not performers at all, have no training in the art forms whatsoever and who perform and even teach under the guise of professionalism. I don't mean for a minute to deprecate the work of the beginner or the amateur, whose work we need and who should be encouraged. I take issue only with the claims of professionalism from the totally unequipped. These people are damaging to the growth of Mime and Pantomime. In time, an enlightened theatre audience will correct this condition, but until then, this damage will be formidable.

Mime has become chic this year. In the do-it-yourself panorama of the pop-art mediums it is enjoying something of a fad. I don't think that this popularity is based on anything real, nor that it will last or increase. Being an American Mime performer in the United States at this time in history is a committment rather akin to becoming a Trapist Monk in Italy in the 17th Century. And I see no reason that that should meaningfully change in the future. Or, said in another way, the theatre is kept alive not by popularity, or the psychological necessity of its products, but by the internal need, or compulsion, of its practitioners to practice it in order to lead a creative life.

Q. How is American Mime received today by critics and audiences?

PJC. The American Mime theatre has become hunchbacked with accolades. We are known as a "serious attraction," an artistic success. Loosely translated this means our work is generally not as bad as most of the professional theatre, we believe in what we are doing and have money trouble. There is a great confusion when we talk about critics. The primary function of a critic is to aid the artist and for this he must be armed with enough information concerning the form itself and the aim of the artist to bring his heightened perceptions to bear on the creative product against his personal standards of excellence. The function of a reviewer is to apprise the community at large of the general experience that the creative product affords. The function of any performing art is to touch and move the audience, to create a spiritual enrichment. Any performing art has potentially the capacity to do this. It is seldom achieved because most people, Mimes included, don't do what they do very well.

Q. Where does The American Mime Theatre go from here?

PJC. Straight uphill. The mimes at The American Mime Theatre practice this Medium as a way of life. They not only study, perform, teach, and create the material for the repertory, but they administer all the business of The American Mime Theatre and American Mime, Inc. We spent the first 15 years of our life developing our Medium. Now we are committed to the evolution of a superior creative product and the promotion of this Medium throughout the world.

An artist reflects appearances. The artist is living his own appearance.

I'm simply mirroring things from observation.

Children, Animals, and Clowns.

"What I'm doing now is pouring the cup into you," Sam
said as we sat down for the interview, *"So that you may pour
it again with the symbols we call words."* Morroccan-born
mime, Samuel Avital has made Boulder his home because *"it
is a good womb for me to grow in."* Sam dedicates his art to
God for the purpose of giving joy and faith to others. After
years of study under the foremost masters of the time (Etienne
Decroux, Jean-Louis Barrault, and Marcel Marceau). Often
penniless and without a friend in a strange land, Sam has
become rich with experience and willing to share what he
has learned.

Speaking in uncertain English, his words flow like a river
of inspiration, not always in a logical sequence, but often to
the point. In this improvisational innerview (preceded by
meditation), the interviewer decided to leave untouched the
spontaneous, though at times unrelated flow of words as the
silent artist himself uttered them.

I. The Mime Workshop—"The Laboratory of Self"

In the workshop, in the beginning, we imitate animals. That's simple. But later on, you have to find that animal consciousness in you and develop it. You find the center of movement of that animal, and everyone will recognize which animal you are becoming.

In the workshop we isolate different parts of the body physically and psychically to sew them all together. . . so that the elbow can kiss, that you can hear with the eye or you can eat with your nose, and smell with your mouth. Reverse the whole experience, the total exploration, in order to learn, to see not only with eyes, but with the whole body. I'm not a teacher, I'm like a shepherd—just to aim students in the right direction, not to tell them where to go. I like to give individual attention. I must have personal contact with my students. I am not a minister, I am not a doctor, I am not a professor, I am not a Ph.D., or LSD, or IRT or BMT.. . It's not at all a conventional idea of a student-teacher relationship. I am there to learn also. I want to share experience.

You have to train intuition. Concentration is being with what you do now. If you pay attention to what you are doing now, it prepares you for the next moment. There is no later because the next later is the present. There is no philosophy in my workshop because the people who are gathered together there are vibrating to me what to do. No session is similar to another.

In the workshop, we learn how to express things with one part of the body. For instance, sometimes we practice making half of the face sad and half of the face happy. One hand will be doing one activity, and the other hand will be doing the opposite activity. Or one leg wants to walk and the other leg doesn't move. So that you find a certain harmony or balance. So you need a lot of control in mime, and it takes time to exercise and practice. Experience is all language. What happens in the class must be experienced, I cannot describe it to you. Please, come and experience it. When you find that experience is all language, you begin to discover a whole new aspect of life.

Sometimes I create accidents in class, in order to find out how to prevent an accident. But after awhile you find a certain system in you that tells you how to fall and what part of the body to fall with, with what rhythm to fall.

The student has to learn to express one thing by itself, then two, three, four, five, six. . . to put them together to make up a sentence, a verb. And when I say verb, I am thinking of the movement verb. That is learning to speak with the body—but the body is speaking already, we are just unaware of it. When you see how a person walks you know immediately who he is. You can see this in anyone, just look. You learn how to mirror the higher self. Sometimes the reflection is so strong, it's unbelievable. I know my audience at that moment.

There are no voyeurs in my classes. . . If someone asks if they want to come and watch—no sir. Everyone must participate. We explore sound and ritual dances to find out the root of what is dancing or what it is to speak. We put ourselves in a state where there is no speech and we have to express ourselves in a new language. And it's amazing, people understand. You must invent, but before you do that you must put yourself in a state of perception. To prepare the body to listen to you. It's an instrument. The human body is a map and we have to know every corner of it.

For those who are really curious, who are seeking the truth, they'll find it. That's the difference between the theatre department at a university and my work. Because here I say to people, "enough"—enough Shakespeares and Molieres, now let's be Shakespeares and Molieres. We can. We are ready for that. Which means I want the actor to create and to do his mask, but not with make-up. You become one with what you are portraying. And that's why it's fascinating when an audience is seeing an actor like that, they think he's God. I want to bring theater back to its religious, spiritual root, that's what I'm after. And this needs training.

Your mind controls your body. It sends a little telegram to me to move myself in rhythm. The student has to learn to direct himself—I cannot direct him. He has to develop it himself. For instance, suppose we want to convey dancing to get the whole audience to dance. We're not going to force the dance, we must seduce them to dance. We must first experience the dance, and that experience will sweep the audience into dancing. It's contagious. In order to be contagious, you have to burn with the energy: To flow with water and not be drowned.

For instance, people do not know how to walk. They take it for granted. In the workshop, a student taught me something fantastic. We were talking about walking and he explained that the feet are flat, that they touch the ground evenly, and that a wheel of an automobile is round.

While the round wheel is rolling, the part which is on the earth is always flat. Similarly, while our feet are in motion and not touching the earth, they move in a circle just like the wheel. Any movement that is not circular is not natural.

II. The Philosophy Behind the Silent Art

Everyone is unique, and I'm after that, to find that uniqueness, and kick it up and out so that person realizes it and gives it away to others. Be with me one second and suppose you are walking on the street with a smile on your face. You meet a man and you are smiling and he is smiling, and you both keep that smile and spread it to others. So in the space of five minutes there will be a hundred people smiling.

Children for me are great teachers. Everyone is my teacher. Children, animals, and clowns—in these three things you can find the whole world. I want some day to put on the stage the man who dies laughing. He is laughing so he is not dead. So tragic.

My philosophy is to eat only when I'm hungry, to drink only when I'm thirsty, and to forgive quickly anyone who harms me. These are three things I have based my life on.

I'm just simply mirroring things from observation. Many things from my repertory, for instance "The Banana Man," were suggested by little children. After a show, I asked some children, "What do you want me to do for you now?" They said, "Oh, eat a banana, fly to the moon and walk on it." (By the way, the moonwalk is a mime technique—we had it in mime before they ever got to the moon). The children teach me and I give it back to the audience. I am mirroring the gluttony which is in us.

If you walk and you feel fear, it is obvious you will be attacked because your rhythm of walk is

Once the tool is sharpened enough, you can sculpt the fantasy in space.

19

different when you are sure of yourself. You should not let the rhythm of the city sweep you up like a downstream river.

When I performed "the insect" in New York, some people came backstage and stared at me. And I asked, "What's happening?" And they said, "We just wanted to check if you are really an insect or a human being." I asked, "What do you do?" and they said, "We're psychiatrists."

When alot of people are focusing on you on the stage it's holy. The more you give, the more you are rich. God is an experience and you cannot talk about it.

When I sit down to interview people, I am discovering the whole world. People are pouring into you. We are trees, this is a Cabbalistic conception. But the roots are up. But they're hidden. Look at a drawing of the human brain, the little veins and nerves, it's like a tree.

Today we cannot lie anymore. My theater is not just a physical theater, it's psycho-physical. My grandfather once told me, "You know when a baby is born, he is given a certain amount of words to use in his lifetime. When you learn to talk to people, you begin to use these words. So every word you use is out of the total. So if you speak too much, one day you might find yourself mute. So be economic with words. That influences my art-form, that story. Speak only when necessary.

In our Jewish culture in Morrocco we have days that we don't speak. We fast from speech. Once I worked in a camp and I introduced this to the kids in the camp, a very noisy camp, and we all had one day of silence. And they got excited about it. You should have seen that camp. People walked so peacefully and they wanted to prove to themselves that they could do it. It was a beautifully quiet day.

I was in Ohio. . . where I was staying at a friend's house and after dinner I went walking and suddenly found myself in darkness. So I went looking for the light switch. All at once I found myself in emptiness, in open space and I let myself go, I surrendered and relaxed. I rolled down 25 or 30 wooden steps, but I didn't realize it at the moment. I totally relaxed. Once I got to the bottom, someone turned on the lights. Upstairs, they looked down at me and asked, "What are you doing down there?" I said, "I just got here." "Are you okay?" they asked. Only later did I understand what happened, that when you find yourself in total emptiness of space, surrender, relax, because whatever is going to happen will happen.

This story I once told to my students, and when you convey stories to people sometimes things happen. One day a girl came and knocked on my door with great excitement. She told me that this is what had occurred: "I had a party at my house and the people are still there but I came running here to tell you this. I was leaning on the railing of my balcony and suddenly it collapsed and I fell two stories to the grass. At that moment when I fell, it passed through my mind to totally relax and I did." She didn't suffer even a scratch, though all her friends panicked. (This happened a year and a half after she heard Sam's story.)

I will tell you one experience in Paris one day. My hair was long before the hippies because I didn't have the money to go to the barber and if I had any money, I would go and eat and give something to my stomach so I could survive. So one of those days, I had been really hungry for a few days and I was sitting on a Champs-Elysees bench, very tired and sad. A blind man with a cane came by, tapping with his cane on the ground. And a crippled man went by. Then an old woman with a wheel-chair passed, and a child with paralyzed legs. It was a parade prepared for my eyes. I don't know how long I stayed there. Suddenly, I got up, and I walked down the street and I thought, "There are people who can't see, and I see. There are people who can't hear, and I hear. There are people who are crippled, and I am full, total." So I got to be happy. The stomach will be filled, don't worry.

I was walking like that, and I got to the Montparnasse and I came to a bakery. I saw this cake in the window (I wrote even a poem about that cake) and I looked at that cake with such alarm, I was thinking, "If only it would come into my stomach. . ." with such seriousness. Suddenly, there was a hand on my shoulder, and a man who I knew vaguely said "Hey Samuel, come on, come on, eat some croissants and take some home." I said, "No, I don't need it." And he said, "Take it, take." I didn't have any words in my mouth, so I said, "Thank you," and he went. And I walked out of the store eating the croissant, and I looked at the cake, and I smiled such a miserable smile. . . that was one day in my life in Paris.

(Recorded by Scott Gibbs)

Expansions of Now

I am interested in a "CORPS" of Mime, one body, with one group consciousness, after the classical training one gets to find his own way. I look for a certain "Totality" in the theater work, a totality of being, an ability to be part of the "Corps" that makes a Unity, a oneness of action, honest and believable. In other words, I want my actors to be engaged to believe in what they do, with the utmost truth; this is the reaction to the tired conventional theater, in which there is no participation, where you are being treated to be there, and the actor serves you, with words; words, without involving you into the action.

We live in times where one wants to take our audience into the experience without fear, to enlighten the spectator, electrify him, so that he will carry with him some kind of knowledge that makes him rich, and raise by this his level of consciousness, to become more aware of his environment and his friends. Therefore, we train actors to be God-like, to master the situations in action, to be enough open to go to his audience and confront him as he is in a human rapport, and not as a number in a computer.

In order to do that I wish my actors to know themselves enough to lead an action under different rhythms, forms, to a climax or more. Our workshops then are leaded to that ultimate goal, and with great perserverance, and hard work the students begin to open more of themselves and act accordingly to the scenes that are on stage at that specific moment.

The workshop-theater-laboratory is concerned with developing the harmony of mind and body through the techniques of mime; increasing imagination and self-awareness of movement, actions and reactions with the control of the mind. Through this psycho-physical approach we explore the time, space, object, subject of the self, and environment, and we act while the muscle, married with breath, is moving to the command of the mind.

The totally aware theater actor of today is more concerned than ever with the great possibilities of this work, this theater life approach of no division between actor and audience. He will eliminate the long-time passivity of the spectator, thus, the union of actor-audience, mind-body, individual group is achieved through this training encounter which can apply to everyone in our everyday life. We want to bring a healthy dish to the new audience of the new age.

We see that we come back always to our source, essence. This art of silence has taught me personally how to live among men and women, and these experiences I am interested in sharing with my students on a purely human level.

With this suggestive work, with the self and with practical training, IT becomes later, when the student is a master of an auto-suggestive work to be used everyday, and which will sharpen our awareness with the use of all our human abilities and potential in every walk of life, here and now, in this vast stage of our being.

Dallas
February 10, 1971

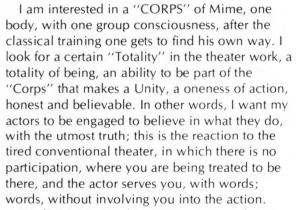

A Word of Welcome—To the student of UMW

WELCOME, is a beautiful appropriate word to tell you, to this space in which we will share together some time, "I" thank you for BEING here, without you "I" will not BE here. Blessings, to "YOU".

It is the time to spend with our inmost SELF, to work honestly as we walk along, so be prepared to WORK hard, with your totality, body and mind, it is joyful, we learn by doing, experiencing, your attitude must ZOOM to concern, practice in word and deed, committment and dedication to the WORK.

Keep a book of notes to record your work, you will need it some time later. In time feel free to ask, speak to the point when you utter a word, measure your words, and use the words with a minimum as you can.

A harmonious relationaship between you and me is of great importance, so that the learning experience will be fulfilled, feel free to talk to me your heart in any matter, or be with my presence to give me the great opportunity to serve you to my best of abilities.

As you perceived by now, this work is spiritually integrated in the teaching of this art-form of MIME, the way I see fit to impart it unto you, beyond name, attribute, or dogma, that is why it is so important to BE NOW HERE.

Avoid thinking negatively while working in this space, it will contribute to the harmony of the whole, and add to to the joy of explorinig some

beautiful areas in our SELVES, I trust you to KEEP this attitude all ways facing you constantly.

If you work with me here more than one period of the workspace, you will be led to what we call "Personal Program" to embrace you more in depths in some areas of your interest, IF you ask for it, and know HOW.

No missings whatsoever of the sessions, it is like a chain, so await the unexpected, and be surprised at everything that might happen to you while working, I am here only to assist and serve you, and remind you few of the things you NEED to know.

With all that is here in mind, let us dedicate our time to that SELF, with concern, joy, harmony and LOVE.

Samuel Avital

General Outline of the Mime Work

Sept. 1971-1974

This contains some of the topics studied between September 1971 to 1974.

Recorded direct from our sessions at work, and reflecting language, expressions, and ways we work. For those who worked here with us, it will serve as hints, or keys to the experience itself. For others, not encountering our work from within, it might seem poetic, but all here is based on actual experience and meaning.

We live in times when we can't lie anymore.

1. MOTION/STILLNESS

>*"Many of us think that moving a lot is mime. We go through that to come to the point that not moving is mime."*

2. STACATTO AND SLOW MOTION

>*"It is not to do it, it is what is happening in the process of doing it. This is what mime is about."*

3. UNDULATION—PROCESSION ENCHAINE

>*"Mime is like moving in water, has the rhythm of fire, and is bound to the earth."*

4. PARALLELS

>*"Mime makes the invisible, visible and the abstract, concrete."*

5. SNAIL MOVEMENT

>*"Perfect movement is not enough. If must be perfect spirit, too."*

6. ANIMAL WORK

>*"The qualities of every animal can be found in Man."*

7. STICKS AND MASKS

>*"The stick is only a pretext for working on yourself." "Your mask is a reflection of how you feel about yourself."*

8. BASES AND FIXATIONS

>*"I swear to do the possible and only the possible."*

9. SENSES

>*"These are five senses. What about the other ninety-five?"*

10. TRIPS

>*"Do it like doing it for the first time."*

11. GRAVITY

>*"Science fights gravity, mime works with it."*

12. LEADERS

>*"The leader and follower are a circle."*

13. EMPTYING/WORDS AND MOVEMENT

>*"Empty yourself so you can be filled."*

1. MOTION/STILLNESS

"Many of us think that moving a lot is mime. We go through that to come to the point that not moving is mime."

Walk neutral around the space. Freeze on a signal. Feel the motion in no-motion. "Stop and see what is happening."

Freeze into attitudes from statues or paintings you have seen. Don't let the eyes move. Eyes fixed.

Become/actualize different feelings with the whole body. Then relate to other people in the space in a completely spontaneous way. No planning.

"Become a letter in space." (The letter anger or joy, for example)

Work with the aspect of sometimes planning what your form will be before you strike the attitude. Make your body listen to you.

Work with one person moving around and the whole group following him according to his rhythm, not mirroring him. Direct an attitude toward him. Carry the attitude according to his rhythm.

Work in small groups and develop a series of photographs in which each person is added, one at a time, until it is complete. Return to a neutral line between the pictures.

Become aware of how you apply no-motion in everyday life. When? Where? Learn to apply it consciously. Observe it in animals. They know to stop and listen with the whole body.

Points of Emphasis
    Immediate balance
    Proper amount of energy in assuming
        attitude
    Eyes fixed
    Don't hold the breath
    Projecting the feeling

Quotes
    "Freeze into the essence."
    "Direct translation of thought into form"
    "Ex-pression"
    "Enthusiasm of the moment"
    "Be your own mirror."

Something must be emptied before it can be refilled.

30

Many of us think that moving a lot is mime. We go through that to come to the point that not-moving is mime.

1. MOTION/STILLNESS
Empty Page

2. STACATTO AND SLOW MOTION

"It is not to do it, it is what is happening in the process of doing it. This is what mime is about."

Begin by making a traject (a specific line of movement through space) and walk through it until it becomes a "physical mantra".

Work the traject in stacatto rhythm. Break down the everyday movement into pieces of movement like a camera lens opening and closing. Walking in stacatto send a telegram to one part of the body and move it. Be careful the movement is not tense. Breathe the movement.

Work the voice with the body neutral. Work "Chopped meat sound". Take one sentence or phrase and repeat it very stacatto. Let the sound begin to move the body stacatto in a third trip style. Let the whole body become involved. Continue to chant while the body is moving. Let the chant fade out while the body continues in stacatto movement. Let the chant continue inside your head.

Then work the traject again in a stacatto rhythm. Contrast this by freezing and going into a very slow, fluid motion. Continuous motion at a constant speed. Keep the body relaxed. What is the effect that this rhythm has on the breathing?

Keep the image of an automation or a camera lens opening and closing for stacatto movement.

Keep the image of a dish moving in water or that nothing is happening for slow motion.

Points of Emphasis

    Continuous motion, constant speed for slow motion.

    Broken rhythm but at constant speed for stacatto.

    Don't be carried by the chanting and moving together. You must carry it.

    Know which part of the body you are going to move in stacatto.

    What is the process of the stacatto movement?

    Move one part at a time.

    Stop between each movement.

    Remember to breathe.

Quotes

    "Stop and realize between two steps"

    "You move but you don't move"

    "Take two thousand years to go there"

    "Let the movement teach you to breathe"

    "Conquer the world, but in a relaxed way"

    "Une chose a la fois"

Note

In the study of slow motion it is important to remember that every exercise and movement done should be practiced slow motion, particularly in the learning stages. Slow motion is more than a technique, it is a whole way of life.

33

It is not to do it, it is what is happening in the process of doing it. This is what mime is about.

2. STACATTO AND SLOW MOTION
Empty Page

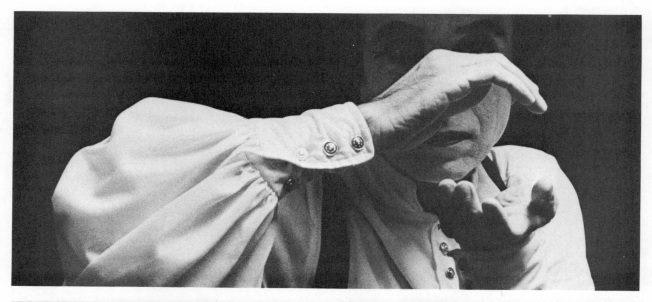
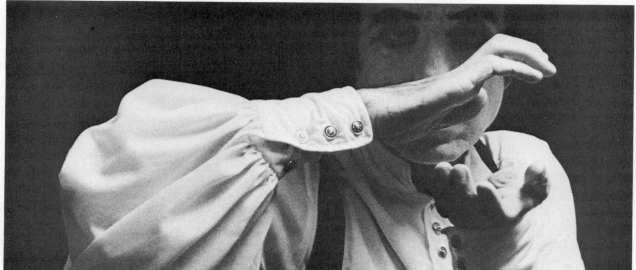
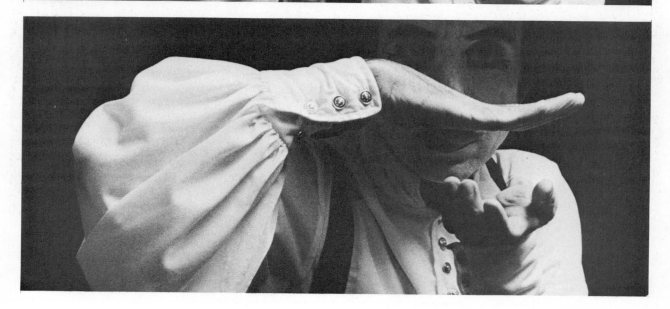

3. UNDULATION—PROCESSION ENCHAINE

"Mime is like moving in water, has the rhythm of fire, and is bound to the earth."

One part follows the other in a continuous succession. Have the image of a train going into a tunnel, a serpent and a cat. Work the two planes of the body: The plane profondeur and transverse plane.

Begin with 75% of the weight on the front foot and 25% on the back foot. Face front. Knees are bent. Raise each part of the body successively backwards (head, neck, chest, waist, etc.) until the weight is shifted 75% on the back leg and 25% on the front leg. The back leg is bent. Beyond the movement of the chest, the body does not go up anymore.

Work the undulation on the transverse plane. The same applies in regards to the upward movement of the body and the distribution of the weight. Keep the body on the exact plane. Do not be forward or backward in any part. Have the image of the body in a sandwich.

Undulation in a free form. Keep the image of water. Let the movement breathe you.

Begin undulating each separate part of the body (Head, shoulders, arms, torso, etc.) Do this in a free way however the movement and image suggest. Think fluidity and stay relaxed. Do this on the space and then walking. Be careful not to neglect the legs and torso.

Work with another person, undulating around each other. Give and take space. Don't manipulate each other. Do this in a very free way with no planning.

What does this movement say to you? What is the sound this movement brings forth? The sound must come as a result of this movement.

Undulate on all fours and work with the rhythms of the cat letting the movement of the undulation transform you into the cat.

Work the stillness of the cat. Work the animal pride and the ability to instantly change rhythms. Work the facial mask. Find the cat in you and let it be manifested. Relate with another cat.

Work with a group following one person's rhythm and freezing when he does. Note how the animal work has sharpened the awareness.

Points of Emphasis
    Continuous movement on the body.
    No planning.
    Relax but don't let go.
    No manipulation when working with
       another.
    Slow motion.

Quotes
    "Swim in the space"
    "Undulate into each other's space"

You are the picture. Do you see the picture?

Mime is like moving in water, has the rhythm of fire, and is bound to the earth.

3. UNDULATION—PROCESSION ENCHAINE
Empty Page

A relaxed hand is the most beautiful.

4. PARALLELS

"Mime makes the invisible, visible and the abstract, concrete."

Begin by placing the hands on a wall and moving the body from left to right. Feel the adaptation the body makes to this fixation. Feel the relative movement between the hands and the whole body.

Then work the wall on the empty space. Feel the movement from the center of the body. Some important points to remember are:

1. Erase the feet. Their work should not be seen.
2. Become aware of what parts of the body are moving parallel.
3. Keep the hands on the same plane.

With a partner, work walking along a wall, mirroring each other's movements.

Stand zero, raise arms from wrist to the level of navel. Push down with flat palms and raise the body up on the toes. Keep the heels kissing.

ROPE PULLING

Stand in second position. Raise the hand to the level of the navel. Hands holding rope which goes parallel to the earth. Elbows are bent. Study the parallel of this movement. The center of this movement is not in the chest but in the navel. The hands pull across the body while the pelvis moves in the opposite direction, shifting the weight from 75% on one foot to 25% on the other. Hand over the back of the rope (the weight is not 25% on the back foot) crosses over the other hand, then the other hand grasps the rope in the same place as in the beginning. In this process the weight is again shifted to 75% on back leg and 25% on front (front being the direction from where the rope is coming).

Climbing stairs

Grab rail at level of the head. Hands are fixed. Place one foot slightly forward on the ball of the foot. Raise the body up on that ball to its limit and as the body goes up the hands go down the same distance as the body goes up. As the body goes back to flat foot, the hands stay fixed. No echo. Hands grab rail again as other foot moves forward on its ball and this process repeats itself.

Work pushing and pulling simultaneously with the body. Pull with the right hand, push with the left. Then pull with left, push with the right. Work this on the transverse plane and on the plane profondeur. Observe the shifting of the weight and the line of the body.

Work with a partner, mirroring each other's movements.

Points of Emphasis

Move from the pelvis.
Keep the pelvis on one geometrical line.
Keep the hands on one geometrical line.
The footwork is invisible.
Do one thing at a time.
Find the center of the movement.

Quotes

"Let the movement breathe you."
"Mime is like moving through water."
"Before we go forward, we go backward."

Mime makes the invisible, visible and the abstract, concrete.

4. PARALLELS
Empty Page

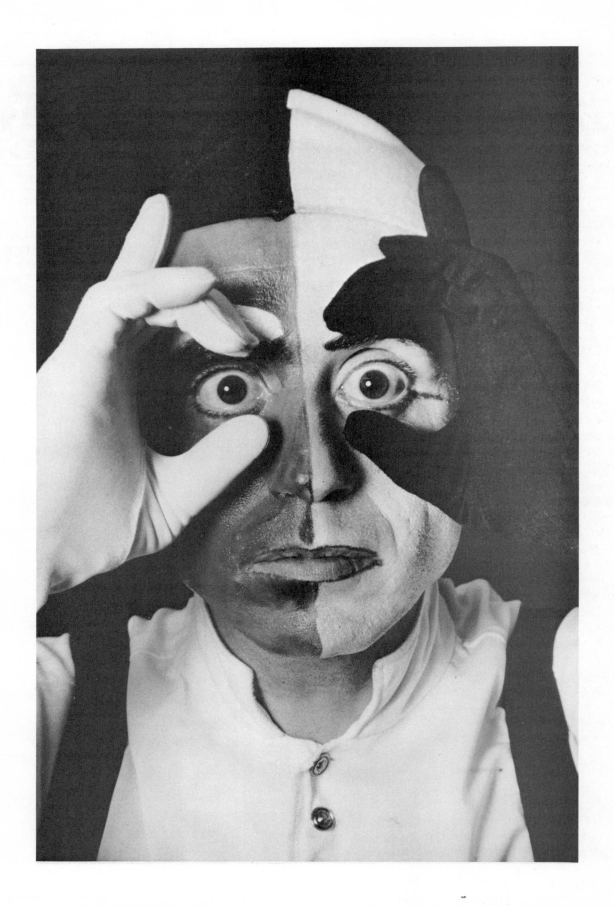

"Black and White" by Avital. Emphasizes contrast and the tragic divisions of mankind.

5. SNAIL MOVEMENT

"Perfect movement is not enough. It must be perfect spirit, too."

Begin in a relaxed zero, motionless. Feel the plumb line of the body (a straight line from the top of the head to the ground, running through the body). Feel each part of the body as a part of a tree, blowing in the wind. Work this in slow motion.

Feel the withdrawal of each part. This is done by contracting and immediately withdrawing each part of the body. One part of the body withdraws and the rest of the body follows and adapts. Work each part of the body from head to foot in all directions using this technique and find the limits of each part. This is called the snail cycle.

Feel the withdrawal in the entire body. Become aware of the line of the withdrawal. Be able to draw that line on a sheet of paper. Withdrawal may also be done from a wall so that the point of withdrawal can be clearly marked.

Have the image of walking in the wind, primitive amoeba or sticking that part of the body in hot water.

Then divide into couples and work this with one person closing the eyes and withdrawing at the place on the body where the other is touching (pelvis, shoulder, etc). Both must participate in the withdrawal at the moment of touch.

Then work with one person using the withdrawal to cause the other to lie down by touching different parts of the other's body. In order to do this properly the person touching must assume the exact attitude of the person being put down to see where the weight is. "See the world through that person's eyes." After the person is lying down flat on his back then get them back up. In doing this exercise it is important for the person being touched not to assist for the sake of getting into a more comfortable attitude. Be sincere with where you are being touched. Take the withdrawal to its limit—no more, no less.

Points of Emphasis
> Contract at point of withdrawal and immediately relax during the echo of the withdrawal.
> Let the body adapt to that part which is withdrawing.
> Slow, slow motion.
> Sharp, short withdrawal. Long and smooth echo. Don't kill the echo. Let it go on to immortality.
> Line of the Movement.

Quotes
> "If there is effort in the movement, this is not the work."
> "There are three types of withdrawal: Animal (gross), human (mediocre) and divine (perfect)."
> "Every movement has a line, a breath and a center."

Youth is not an age—it is a fluidity of being.

Perfect movement is not enough. It must be perfect spirit, too.

5. SNAIL MOVEMENT
Empty Page

6. ANIMAL WORK

"The qualities of every animal can be found in Man."

Before we begin the study of the animal there are some things that must be considered.

1. What are some of the unique qualities that animals share?
   a. Highly developed senses
   b. Motion/stillness
   c. Ability to focus
   d. Walk on all fours
   e. Will not attack unprovoked
2. What is the center of movement of the animal you are working?
3. The qualities of all animals are contained in every human being and everyone has a specific animal counterpart.
4. From where does the sound of that animal come?
5. When working animals only 75% of you must become that animal. The rest of you must remain the viewer so that potential accidents can be avoided.

Begin animal work through the process of self-exhaustion or emptying. Explode with the body in a totally free way and on a signal you go immediately back to a neutral zero. Explode using sound with the movement. Exhaust yourself totally, then lie down and relax. Visualize a pinpoint of light, which is yourself, becoming larger and larger which is reborn into the animal that you have chosen. Do not open your eyes. Be born as that animal. Be with that animal's movement. Assume an attitude of that animal and slowly open the eyes. Work the face of the animal. Focus the attention on each section of the body from head to toe. Move as the animal under different states of mind. What is the sound and movement of the animal when it is:

1. Afraid
2. Eating
3. Searching for food
4. Courting
5. Playing
6. Sleeping

Find a mate that you are attracted to, according to his movement, and become involved in the above activities with them. Return to your human consciousness through the same process of relaxing and visualizing a pinpoint of light that becomes you.

Related Exercises

Take a group of five to ten people and place one person in the center. Others form a circle around him and try to reach him without being seen. If he sees them they must return to their starting point. Excellent for developing reflexes on both sides.

Try walking like a cat in the morning.

Find a logical process of development from different rhythms we work into different animals. Example: Undulation into cat.

Work acting lightning. Stand at zero and instantly explode out with one part of the body and immediately back to zero like nothing happened, completely relaxed.

Points of Emphasis

Keep that 25% watching yourself.
Respond as that animal would.
Be able to go instantly out of that animal and back into yourself.

Quotes

"It is not just to do it, but rather what is your state of mind when you do it."
"Act lightning."
"Whenever you feel yourself losing your center, fix your eyes."
"Cat consciousness."
"Like a flash of fire."

The qualities of every animal can be found in Man.

6. ANIMAL WORK
Empty Page

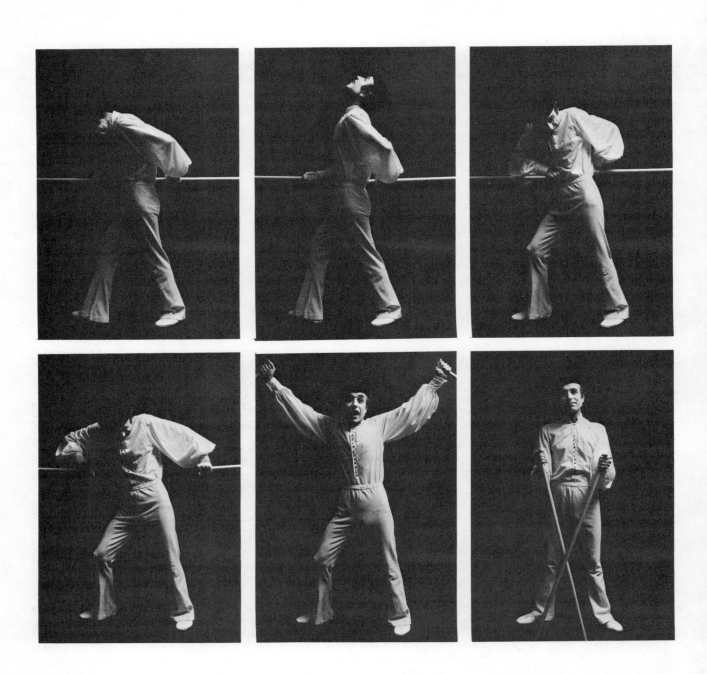

7. STICKS AND MASKS

"The stick is only a pretext for working on yourself."

"Your mask is a reflection of how you feel about yourself."

Masks

What is a mask? Consider all the possible forms a mask can take besides a facial mask (the clothes you wear, a car you drive).

Express an emotion with the whole body. Let every part of the body express that feeling without the help of the face.

Go through your everyday routines with your mask on and feel the difference in the way your body responds. Find the use of your whole body in your everyday routines.

Go to different environments with your mask and study how the mask heightens the use of the whole body. For example, a zoo, a museum, watching a movie.

Work with the whole group interacting together in different environments. Example: A party.

Work moving in total darkness with the mask. Note the eye and head movements. Become aware of the power of stillness in this. Listen with your whole body. Economy of movement in this work is very important.

ON MAKING MASQUES

You need a form or mold, and material to make a mask.

A. The mold can be:
1. A clay model or mannequin's face — Sculpt a face with a modeling clay, may be a cardboard box of an appropriate size.
2. Someone's face — or your face, preferably a neutral face.
3. A plaster of paris mold, requires making a negative of a face, then pouring in plaster of paris, peeling away the negative when plaster is dry.

B. Material
1. Paper mache. Several layers of strips of paper dipped in flour-water paste. Can add a commercial clay mache for strength.
2. Buckram. One or two large pieces to cover face. Press and model them to conform to face or to contours of the mold.

A mime must be more acutely aware of Life than the average man.

53

3. Celastic. Handle like buckram, but dip in acetone to soften.

All these materials can be cut, sanded, glued, gesso-ed, painted, sprayed, stippled, etc. . .

C. Instructions:

Cover hair with a stocking or band, put towel around neck. Coat face with vaseline, especially on brows or lashes. Use buckram (can also be a mask right here) pieces dipped in water, or splint material dipped in water, and mold pieces to the face, leaving nose holes and dip under the chin — otherwise mold will be too shallow. Coat inside with vaseline. Shake plaster into bowl of water and mix. when it is consistency of a slightly thin pea soup, pour into inside of negative mold, let dry, and paint it white, not shiny.

The mask should be neutral, egg mask; care of the eyes cutting afterwards, and nose holes.

In making the mask, become aware of your thoughts, work on it in a quiet meditative mood, every movement is important, nourish the thoughts of: what is a mask, and what for, a face? or a covering of a face? or a revealing identity of the self? meditate on WHY in this culture only the face and hands are naked.

Above all, enjoy in the DOING of it, and face it with harmony.

Points of Emphasis for Masks
> Study the movement of the head.
> Don't do like everyday. If you want, want with your whole body.
> Use a completely neutral mask.
> Note how the face feels when you remove the mask after working with it for a long period ot time.
> Eyes should be fixed when working in darkness.

Sticks

Stand in zero. Throw stick from one hand to the other. Keep the line of the stick perpendicular to the earth.

Hold the stick in front of the body with one hand. Release it with that hand and immediately replace it with the other hand. Stick should not move. The proper amount of energy is important for this.

Hold the stick in both hands, parallel to the earth, throw it in the air and catch it in one hand with a fluid motion. Do not break the flow of the movement.

Hold the stick at one end with both hands. The length of the stick should be above the hands. Let it slide through the hands, catching it at the other end. Return stick to its original position with one swift movement of the hands, keeping faithful to the line the stick is on. It should not bend from side to side.

Work with another person. Each person holds one end of the stick with the other end on the ground. At a certain silent moment you both move and grab the other's stick with your opposite hand while the stick is momentarily suspended in space. As your communication increases with the person the space between you can get larger. Work the exercise with three or four people.

Work the basic combat maneuvers with another person. One person strikes from above, below, right or left. Swing the stick above the other's head and below his feet. The other person blocks with his stick. Feel the way the whole body adapts to the stick. The blows should be made very lightly and the stick should be held with a very relaxed hand.

Take a group of eight to ten people in a circle with one person in the center. The person in the center holds the stick by its end and swings it around passing under the others' feet. They jump over it as it passes under them keeping their knees very relaxed and bent when jumping over the stick.

Points of Emphasis for Sticks
> Be faithful to the line of the stick.
> Use the proper amount of energy.
> Don't panic when jumping over or catching the stick. Be relaxed and ready.
> Breathe with the movement of the stick.
> Work with your stick, don't manipulate it.

Related Exercises

Work with the stick as different objects. Use it as a violin, golf club, telescope, broom. When doing this the emphasis is not on the stick but on the way the body is adapting to the stick. Let the stick become invisible. It is only a pretext for working with the body.

Quotes
> "Minimum of movement, maximum of expression."
> "Full expression, not everyday expression."
> "Like a cat."
> "The stick is an extension of your own body."
> "Make the invisible, visible and the visible, invisible."

*The stick is only a pretext for working on yourself.
Your mask is a reflection of how you feel about
yourself.*

7. MASKS AND STICKS
Empty Page

8. BASES AND FIXATIONS

*"I swear to do the possible and only
the possible."*

Put the feet together on one base and see how the body moves. Find many different ways to move. Have the image of Man before the first step was discovered.

What are the different bases of the body? Begin with one base. How many different attitudes can you assume with one base? Find all the possibilities. It is important to relax in the attitude. You should be able to talk normally at all times.

Work with the body on two, three, four, up to six bases.

Work with another person going through the same process beginning with one base and going up to six bases. Find the common center.

Work this with three, four and five people in the same process.

Centre Fixee

Begin by placing one hand on the space and move towards it, away from it and around it in all directions. Do not bring the hand to you. Go to the hand. Be aware of the adaptation the body makes to the fixation, particularly the shoulder and elbow. The hand and wrist should be relaxed.

Work with both hands individually and held together.

Have the image of the hands on a stick, jail bars or on a table.

Work all the different parts of the body (head, shoulders, chest) in this manner.

Sit and stand with different parts of the body fixed on one plant.

Work with a partner with two parts fixed to each. For example: Both your heads or both your shoulders. Walk around the common center. Don't manipulate your partner in any way.

Work with a small group of not more than four or five. Using the fixed center, find how many posibilities there are for creating physical mandallas with the bodies. Be able to move from one form to another. Keep the common center. Use all the possibilities of the bodies. Examples are: Sitting, standing, lying on backs.

Points of Emphasis

Relaxation of fixation
Adaptation the body makes to fixee
Move slow motion when going around fixee
Invisible work of the feet.

Quotes

"Keep the channels of breath open."
"Mime makes the invisible, visible and the abstract, concrete."

57

What's your name love?

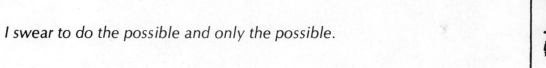

I swear to do the possible and only the possible.

8. BASES AND FIXATIONS
Empty Page

9. SENSES

"These are five senses. What about the other ninety-five?"

Sight

Begin with British flag, holding the eyes in each position and feeling them. Rub hands together and place over the eyes to rest them.

Pick an object in the room and stare at it, completely neutral and relaxed. Keep the object in your focus and blink three hundred times.

With a partner, stare into each other's eyes for a long time. Close the eyes and continue to see the person.

Examine every part of the person's body with the eyes. Look at every pore "like a scientist". Move away from your partner and keep the eyes focused on each other. Move in slow motion. There is a line between your eyes and your friend's. Then close your eyes, spin your body around and go find your partner with the eyes closed. Use your intuition.

Sound

Lie in relaxation and transfer the ears into all the parts of the body. Listen with the elbow, shoulder, etc.

With a partner listen to different parts of your friend's body. With your feet, listen to his feet, tops of each other's heads, spines, fingers.

Walk around the space listening with different parts of the body as the primary sense organ for hearing. Use the nose as ears, elbows as ears. What is the natural attitude of the body when doing this? Don't use contorted attitudes.

Smell

Use the whole body as a nose. Pick a partner and thoroughly examine his body odor while he examines yours. Then with the eyes closed move away from each other and find each other by smell. You must carry that odor with you when you are separated from each other.

Split into groups of five or six and examine everyone in the group with the smell and separate with eyes closed. Get lost in the room. Find your group in the same space it was in when you left. Use your nose. Use your intuition.

Divide into groups. Find the unifying odor of the group. Physicalize that odor in a group improvisation.

Touch

Begin with the body in zero. Perfect stillness. Feel the water in the body become still. Feel the circular motion of the body.

Touch the space around your body with your whole body in different rhythms. Don't use just the hands and arms, but try using the other parts. Be with whatever part of the body is leading you. Caress the space. Try doing this with "stop-action movement" like a camera lense opening and closing. Observe the body. Then form a circle with the whole group and each individual goes into the center, one by one. The person in the center stands motionless, with the hands folded over the chest and heart, eyes open. He begins turning slowly and as he turns the arms unfold slowly. Focus the eyes on the right thumb which is facing up, giving to the heavens, while the left hand is facing down, taking from the earth. Reach a peak and hold it steady. Don't lose control. Then slow down until you again reach a motionless zero with the arms folded as the beginning. While this is done, the group in a circle may move in different directions and recite various chants to heighten the experience.

Take a partner and explore touch in its total sense. Touch the space around each other and then touch each other with all the parts of your body. Avoid any personal or sexual feelings. This work must be done "like a scientist." Just see how the body feels.

Taste

Begin with a series of exercises designed to loosen the jaw.

1. Open and close the jaw rhythmically.
2. Move jaw from left to right.
3. Open and close the lips rhythmically.
4. Meet the teeth rhythmically.

   Experience swallowing in slow motion. Experience swallowing with different parts of the face (eyes, nose, ears).

   Take a partner and focus on each other's face. Let the face become transformed into the face of an animal you identify with. This is done slowly with one part at a time. Emphasis is on the mouth.

   Eat an apple. Before eating, consider every aspect of the apple. The person who planted the seed is considered, the tree. Eat it very slowly and silently. Listen to the jaws work and feel their movement.

Points of Emphasis
Sincerity with what you are doing.
Follow your intuition.
Let that sense you are working with lead
   you.
Let the body adapt to that sense leader.

Quotes
   "It is important to go beyond the senses to a
      higher plane of awareness."
   "Senses are limited in duration by time and
      space."
   "See with the eyes of a scientist."
   "See with the ears."
   "See with the elbow."
   "Make love with the knees."

These are five senses. What about the other ninety-five?

9. SENSES
Empty Page

10. TRIPS

"Do it like doing it for the first time."

These "trips" are particularly effective after any kind of emptying of the self (sound, movement, or warm-up) as a means for developing greater awareness of the body.

Trip# 1

Lie on the back, legs spread about a foot apart, arms at sides, palms up. Close the eyes. Become all the parts of the body, one part at a time (head, ears, eyes, wrists, every part). For example, the whole body is chest or elbow. Work from head to toe and back up again.

Trip# 2

Lie on the back relaxed. Move every part of the body, one part at a time, like Trip# 1 only this time each part moves. The movement is very subtle. Move the part of your body as if for the first time.

Trip# 3

Lie on the back relaxed. Begin by moving the head in a rhythmic way. Gradually, one part at a time, add the whole body until every part is participating. This trip may be started in other parts of the body (hands, feet) but the emphasis is on starting and adding one part at a time. "Build a fire in the body."

Stoned Trip

Lie on the back relaxed. Go through the whole body, isolating and tensing individual parts. Begin with the head, tense it, hold the breath, then let go. That part of the body is like a stone. Keep the rest of the body relaxed. Only tense the part of the body you are working with.

Voyage A L'inconnu

Close the eyes and lie on the back. Picture yourself getting smaller and smaller, until getting enough to climb through one of the openings of the body. You are no bigger than a cell. Observe the blood and organs of the body. You are small enough to travel through the blood stream. Travel to each part of the body and see how it moves (second trip style) from the inside. After you have traveled to and examined every part, emerge through another opening of the body. See yourself getting bigger and bigger until you are your normal size. Stand very slow motion and open the eyes. And be.

TAPPING TRIP

Tapping lightly with hands over different parts of the body, in the following order:

1) shoulders (26 times each)
2) arms
3) hands
4) head
5) scalp
6) forehead
7) temples
8) nose
9) cheeks
10) lips
11) chin
12) chest
13) waist
14) pelvis
15) legs. All the way down and up.

End with Self-Hugging (72 times each). Then five minutes of standing still aware of breathing and how the body feels.

UNDULATING TRIP

Undulating, a slow motion, flowing, fluid. Let the motion teach you how to breathe. Undulate in the following order:

1) head and neck (snake-like)
2) add lips
3) add shoulders
4) add arms
5) add torso
6) the whole body (voluptuous movement)

Then, undulating steps in space, with correct breathing, slow motion, flowing.

Image TWS = Thread-Wind-Stick. TWS—Static You are the Thread, Wind, Stick. TWS—in space, motion

Positive is not necessarily good. Negative is not necessarily bad. They are simply two ends of the stick.

Do it like doing it for the first time.

10. TRIPS
Empty Page

11. GRAVITY

"Science fights gravity, mime works with it."

Begin lying on the ground. Move head right, cheek to the earth and turn pelvis in the opposite direction. Feel the spine. Then do this movement with feet crossed, one on top of the other, do movement with knees drawn up then drawn up and crossed. Arms should be outstretched to the sides. Do the movement three times in both directions with every attitude. After this stand, very slow motion. Feel the plumb line in the body.

Stand motionless.

Begin to sway to the left and right from the center of the body. Eyes are closed. Let the movement breathe. The body should be very relaxed. Let it begin, build and close by its own will. Be aware of the plumb line of the spine (line from middle of ear to the back of foot).

A step is done

Stand zero, motionless, let the body move forward until gravity pulls you to the earth. Let a step be done. It is not a thinking process. Find the edge of your weight. Feel the transition between the vertical and horizontal. The emphasis is on relaxation. The smaller the step is the better. Think of being blown forward by a wind. Do this in all directions. Always return to zero before taking another step.

Drunk walking

Feel the gravity. Still use the return to zero in a very subtle freeze at the station. The emphasis is on keeping an elevation of the chest. Let a step be

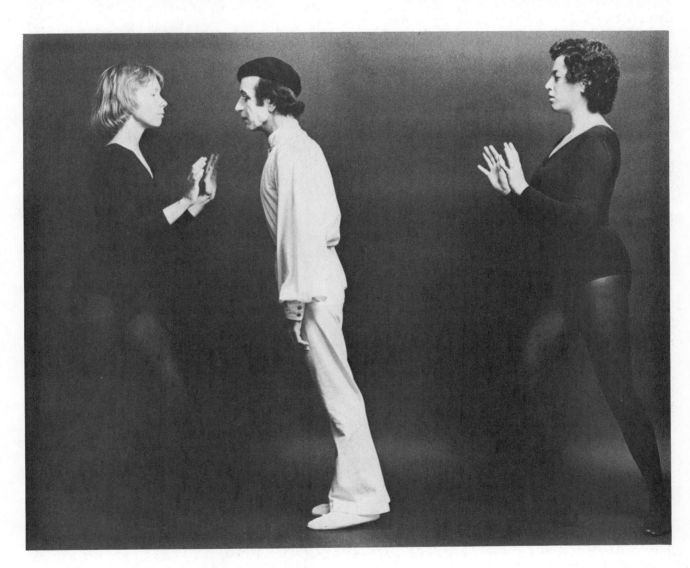

You must go to the edge of reality to show that reality.

69

done. Allow it to happen. The group walks around the room normally and on signal freezes and begins the drunk walking. Feel the difference between the two kinds of movement.

Also, experiment with the body weighing two thousand pounds. Lie on the ground and try to get up.

Then work in pairs. Fall forward and backward and let the other person catch you after you have gone to the edge of your weight. Keep the body erect without any tension. The person who catches must give to the weight of the other and relax, too, for the exercise to succeed.

Work with one person in the center with one person in front and one in back. Let yourself be pushed. Let the energy from the push carry you from one person's hands to the other. In catching, use the thigh for support.

Work this with a group of six to eight people. One person is in the center and is pushed around the circle. The people pushing must communicate where they are sending the center person with their eyes. Don't manipulate.

Go through Trip# 1. Rise in slow motion. Stand zero, motionless for five minutes.

Points of Emphasis
>   In the group work the pusher doesn't manipulate and the pushee doesn't assist.
>   Don't try to plan movement when drunk walking. Let the body go as it will.
>   Let one step be done, not two or three.
>   Be aware of the dramatic moment and play with it. This is emphasized by continually returning to zero.

Quotes
>   "You don't do it, it does you."
>   "Get high on weight, not wine."

When an actor is on stage, the space is the director.

Science fights gravity, mime works with it.

11. GRAVITY
Empty Page

It is not easy to be a mime. First you have to be an alchemist.

12. LEADERS

"The leader and follower are a circle."

Isolate each part of the body and let that part carry you to the edge of your weight. Then let it carry you beyond the edge of the weight so that a step is done. Study how the body adapts to different body leaders.

Work this in all directions: Forward, backward, right and left. Be clear about which direction you are being pulled.

Then work with the leader pulling you back and forth across the room. Note the work of the feet here.

Walk neutral and on a given signal explode with one part of the body leading. Then immediately back to zero like nothing happened.

Work with a partner and let them pull one part of the body with an invisible line. Keep space between you. Use silent communication to indicate what part is being pulled. Practice stillness between the pulls so you can study the attitude of the body.

Points of Emphasis
>Be sincere with the part of the body being led.
>Be aware of the adaptation the body makes to its leader.
>Note the work of the feet.
>Be aware of the dramatic moment when the weight goes over the edge.

Quotes
>"Surprise yourself."
>"A good leader is a good follower."

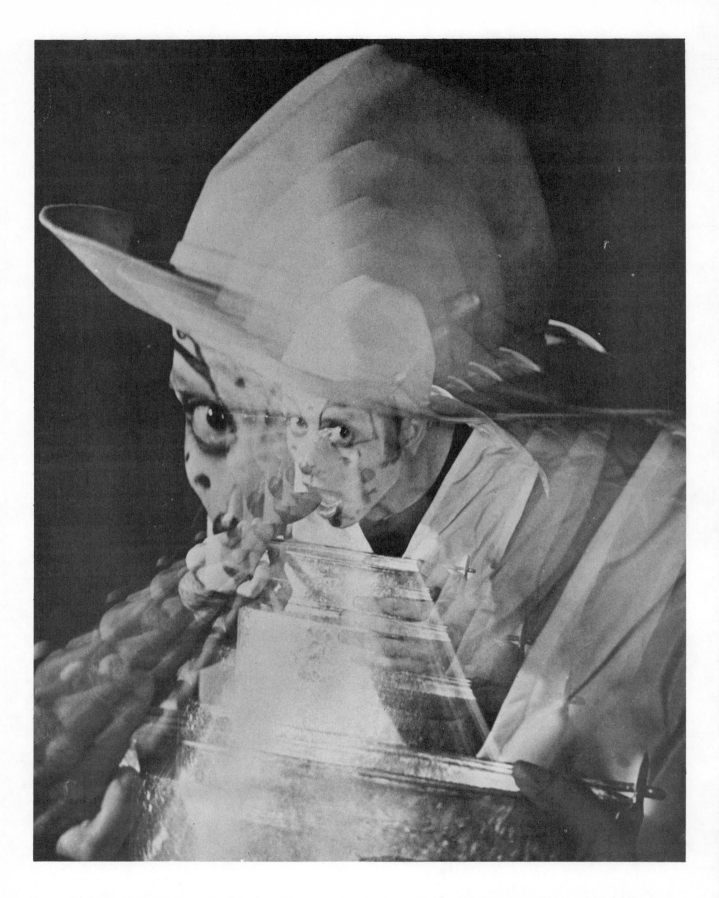

Mime becomes a multidimensional reality which transcends the communication with words that are attached to only 3-sense-dimension that we have.

The leader and follower are a circle.

12. LEADERS
Empty Page

13. EMPTYING/WORDS AND MOVEMENT

"Empty yourself so you can be filled."

Become aware of the point when the air coming out of the throat turns into sound.

Work the different kinds of sound.

1. "Rainbow sound" (soft, loud, soft)
2. "Circular siren sound" (soft, loud, soft, loud, soft)
3. "Chopped meat sound" — Stacatto

Walk in a relaxed way and empty the words. Anything that comes out of the mouth should be allowed to come. Do it in a monotone.

Emphasis here is on no thinking. After doing this alone get into dialogues with other people, objects.

Make an intensive study of the pronunciation of your name. Exaggerate every sound to its total extreme. Let the sound dictate your movement.

Call yourself. Convince another person of your name.

Sing your name. Perform an aria with your name.

Chant your name in a monotone. Speak it at different parts of another person's body.

Have a dialogue using just your name. Know exactly what you are saying. Don't neglect the body.

Have a group of people give one person a sound message by making a unified sound over all parts of the one person's body. For example: Ah, oh.

Through this work one should always put emphasis on the use of the face. Be aware of the work of the jaws and eyes when working with sound.

When working with sound in this way, it is important that the movement comes from the sound. Let your body react and move according to what it hears. Move in a completely free way. Don't get stylized.

When emptying movement the same essential process should be followed as with sound. Take an exercise or movement involving the whole body and repeat it over and over until you reach self-exhaustion. This process is very effective if it follows the emptying sound. Set up a pattern of movement (traject) and follow it over and over, picking an object up at one side of the room and emptying it on the other. Do this like an automaton in a continuous motion, a "physical mantra". When you reach total self-exhaustion, collapse and go through Trip # 1. Then slow motion stand and feel the difference in your mind and body. This work is an excellent introduction to animal work.

Points of Emphasis

When repeating your name, phrase or a movement, keep a monotone.

Do not think.

Do not plan your movement.

Let the sound lead the body as it will.

Quotes

"A non-stop, nonsense journey"

"You want it or you don't want it"

"You must become the caller of the sound, the calling of the sound and the echo of the sound"

There is only one space to write in mime—the stage—you are the letter, you are the brush, and your canvas is your space—your feeling is the color, the intensity of feeling is the intensity of color.

Empty yourself so you can be filled.

13. EMPTYING/WORDS AND MOVEMENT
Empty Page

A Dot in Space

First Session, Tuesday
January 14, 1975
7:30 P.M.

"In the beginning was the word." Before the word there was motion, vibration, movement, the source of all life."
—Samuel Avital

We have labels that signify us as bubbles or units of condensed consciousness; little eggs, little cells, little things that sometimes pretend to know, but in fact it doesn't: but how we get to know each other?

A friend of mine wrote me today that every person is like a drop of water that makes the rain: the rain makes the ocean so everyone is a drop that makes the ocean and here we feel that a lot. It is not just by working. There are a lot of things that will happen to you here in that line because little by little most of us, I think, will come to that change that I talk about.

There is a change to happen in the way of thinking if we want to understand this art form properly. Most of us think words. Even when you repeat a mantra 500 times it is a word, but with an image or something, but very few think images, vision, horizon. This mime should think that. That is why I think that people who are attracted to mime today are very unique people and special; like you. So the way we approach is a kind of an alchemy of transforming that way of thinking words into a relating to the images.

Some people might tell you it is primitive. Ok, let us be primitive. The artist lives in that. Any artist lives in that vision. The musician sometimes might see the notes dancing with each other and then jumping in the space and then disappearing, like Fantasia. It might happen, but how we going to know all these drops together, how we going to make the rain happens into one basket or bunch of cells together mixing up, and drink them in the stomach and digest them somehow. I speak a lot images so you will relate to that too sometime.

But for that we need to introduce each other to each other and we have an explanation for things but we don't have every explanation for everything. Deliberately sometime here you will not be explained certain things, but we are very nice sometimes and divide the work that we do into three aspects.

Every session that we are here we do three aspects of it. First aspect is that understanding of the mind, the intellectual understanding of what we are going to do so that you understand it, so that it will be seated in your consciousness. The next understanding is the experiential understanding, the doing of it, the feeling of it, the heart feeling of it. The third understanding is the application of it, the use of it, how we're going to use it. So there are three phases that we go during the work, during every session. And every session that you are here actually, it's not the workshop.

What you get here, it is material for you to take home and like a cow digest it, vomit it facing you like that beautiful thing and then from there you eat it again and you digest it again and you work.

In other words in the time that we do the middle one, the experiential one here, we should be very concentrated. Concentration span of human beings today is short. When you meet a human being that have ability to concentrate you can't stand around it. It's too much because that person knows what he's doing. So that's the elasticity that we would like to do with our bodies and with our minds. It is very not complicated. So that if you go little by little, follow your steps (if you have any questions you should ask) you should really be with it. OK, the classical question: Who are we? Some of you are hearing this very important for the seventh time but every time it's totally different. Why? Because every one

of you is a fantastic bubble of consciousness that is present here. I feel that there is a very good spirit present with us tonight because we are concentrated. Don't attach the words that I say to my person at all. It's just words that is being said for some purpose; for us together to learn something. That's all. It is a way of talking.

Who do we think we are, before we get to know each other? Any answers are very appreciated. What do you think we are—you are? (group energy, forms of intelligence, imitators of god, here, light, darkness, personalities, the earth) See how many words we say? Go, more words! (Love, imagination, family, purpose, hope, life, fish, we're everything) What was the essence of it? (center, one) Words. We say many words to describe one thing. Sure because we are little drops and every drop drops on the stone or on that house or on that jar or on that thing, but what

You must go down before you go up.

is the form of a drop? (oval, pear-shaped, changing, tear shaped) OK, so we are near. We begin to talk now. It is not love, it is not hope, it is not vision. It is tears, it is oval, a little more essential. OK, we try to develop this a little with you on the tableau and see what we really are.

Now, I need your attention for this explanation because it will follow us all over the workshop and all over our thinking. It is not a dogmatic thing, it is very simple. We talk to the heart; we talk to the logic; we talk to the reason; we talk to every side of us in this kind of explanation that I am going to find out here with you. That is an understanding of, not only what we are, but of the world, how we perceive it. In other mime classes I don't think you get this kind of things. You just go into techniques and work and learn how to pull ropes and that's it, you are a mime. But here it is a basic understanding of the whole selves that we are to know.

Now what is happening? Suppose you are here, we are here and you all look and you see me standing here. What is here standing? How do you see this thing happening? It is like you. It has a form like you. It has everything like you, eyes everything but what is it? (consciousness, mass, piece of form, packaged energy, vibration) What kind of form that you see from this distance? We need this in mime a lot. Mime has a very deep understanding of this. What do you see? (size) but what size do you see me? You see me the shape of you, human form like you, no? But at this distance (a line) A line, OK. A line, to the essence of things: it is a vertical line standing, lying it would be a horizontal line. Just for the understanding. Don't take this as a law of Moses from Sinai ok? Just as an understanding. It will help us very well in the future. For those who can see, this explanation I will repeat. It is one of the keys to understand the multi-dimensional aspect that the mime is looking for (the artist of mime is looking for) and everybody can benefit from it, even scientists because the three dimensional understanding that we have, we work through that too.

It is not enough for us to deal with space because many people think that this is emptiness here, this is foreign. The mime thinks it is both force and void that you can shape, you can sculpt and then make out of that air something solid so to say, that which is invisible, we make visible. This understanding is very important.

OK, now suppose I go one step backward what do you see? (smaller line) I go another step backwards. I am still here but in your perception I am going far back. What is it? (the line gets smaller) You go two miles away. What do you see? (a dot) A dot, the source of the line, thank you that is what we need, a dot. That is what we are—a dot. That is why they say in the old writings: Little human on earth raise your eyes and look, and nobody knows what they are talking about. What do you look, you see the stars and the moon as a dot, therefore you are a dot. It is very important.

Now the intelligence of human beings have found out that when that dot vibrate, there is the law of movement. It vibrates, what is happening? It actually will become bigger no? (draws a spiral) It will become bigger. It just depends the distance, mandala like. Very nice. It is not complicated understanding, everybody knows that, but we need it more, but there are many dots here sitting, a bunch of dots that makes a mass.

Those group of dot are compact, zoomed to something that interests them. It is very solid. It is very group energy that you can do something with it. But what is happening? You saw this line? How a line is formed? By many dots. Many dots together form a line. Is that right? So now we have these dots moving in and out, in any kind of dimension that you want. And what is happening here? Oh wait, it looks like an eye, no? Why our eyes are round? Why the form of the cell is round? That is from where everything begins. That is nice, but here we have this understanding, the intelligence of human beings found the circle and found the boundary of the space between this and this and you have in every machine today this kind of thing.

But now we discovered a line which is opposite to this (draws vertical and horizontal line within circle) In other words this center, that is what all religions are fighting about—for this center. Everybody calls it different names, they fight, they kill each other, and we reverse 5 million years of our evolution. So if we allow every human being to call that center any way he wants, to respect it and then it will happen. When we know that only then we can find this dimension, so to say that we know, and then we can move around in the space of life or movement, that will serve us here and that's what is happening actually, according to some understandings in the life of a person. Every one of us, the thoughts we do, the deeds we do, that is what's happening. That is what's happening in this group. Everyone is a fantastic bubble of good energy, good elements and we are together here just to find out how we are going to channel that. So that is what's happening in life. We have found that if we don't know to do this in life and zoom and become, we have trouble. So from childhood we learn to do that and when we resist to the flow of that, then there is problem. Then there is invention of psychiatrist, there is another gadget there, you go there and you don't know how to do, you zigzag and you hurt and complain and a hundred different volumes about different kinds of things and words and zero and nothing until you learn this movement. This is very important. Any harmonious thing in life, every movement is circular, everything that you do is circular, in your thoughts and in your body, it will happen. That is very simple. But how are we going to become it?

It is good to understand it here intellectually. OK, but we have so many things like this in our bodies and the first organs of perception, we have two like this that we can see—the two eyes that we can see so to say with and teaches that kind of flow circular movement. OK now suppose, that dot in space vibrates with a certain rate. Everyone vibrates in a certain rate that means if some suggestion come—OH NO I do not want to talk about it. You vibrate that. That is why when you get enlightened you giggle. Do not giggle before you get enlightened. It is very interesting. So this is just to understand. What I say here is nothing. It is really nothing. Important is when you go to feel it now.

Thank you for being here.

Samuel

A Fish Story

Once, there was a fish who lived in the great ocean, and because the water was transparent, and always conveniently got out of the way of his nose when he moved along, he didn't know he was in the ocean. Well, one day the fish did a very dangerous thing, he began to think: "Surely I am a most remarkable being, since I can move around like this in the middle of empty space." Then the fish became confused because of thinking about moving and swimming, and he suddenly had an anxiety paroxysm, and thought he had forgotten how. At that moment he looked down and saw the yawning chasm of the ocean depths, and he was terrified that he would drop. Then he thought: "If I could catch hold of my tail in my mouth, I could hold myself up." And so he curled himself up and snapped at his tail. Unfortunately, his spine wasn't quite supple enough, so he missed. As he went on trying to catch hold of his tail, the yawning black abyss below became ever more terrible, and he was brought to the edge of total nervous breakdown.

The fish was about to give up, when the ocean, which had been watching with mixed feelings of pity and amusement, said, "What are you doing?" "Oh," said the fish, "I'm terrified of falling into the deep dark abyss, and I'm trying to catch hold of my tail in my mouth to hold myself up." So the ocean said, "Well, you've been trying that for a long time now, and still you haven't fallen down. How come?" "Oh, of course, I haven't fallen down yet," said the fish, "Because, because—I'm swimming!" "Well," came the reply, "I am the Great Ocean, in which you live and move and are able to be a fish, and I have given all of myself to you in which to swim, and I support you all the time you swim. But here you, instead of exploring the length, breadth, depth, and height of my expanse, are wasting your time pursuing your own end." From then on, the fish put his own end behind him (where it belonged) and set out to explore the ocean.

Practices of Inner Awareness

As you know, there is no attainment to any thing without the constant practice, properly done, steadily, and on times where we build the habit of teaching the body, to become aware of certain things, the main focus should be, to let your OBSERVATEUR all ways at work, without interfering in its work, only then, with long period of practice, one masters that which has been at work, all time.

These are few points to work on constantly, from the Workspace suggestions, that has been given to you, while being here.

1. Fast from words once a week, choose a day, and keep it steady.
2. Fast from food one day a week, same as No. 1.
3. Changing rhythms. If you are walking or doing something fast, let the observateur make you aware of it, and change the rhythm to a slow pace, little by little you will find your own rhythm harmonious with the whole.
4. While you are walking, become all ways aware who is the leaders, what is doing now, follow your legs, breathe with walking.
5. The Cycle-Plastique you learned in the space, once in the morning, once in the evening, until the cycle is regulating your heart beat, peacefully.
6. The cat exercise as you learned it, with the appropriate rhythm, and speed-breathing, you will be energized anew with it all the time.
7. Balance everyday, while tying your shoes, stand on one foot, slightly bent, like a stork, steadily without losing your balance, here also observe the observateur making you balanced without resistance.
8. Stand erect, knees bent slightly, feel weight on the whole foot, and wheel it, rocking from heel to toes, keeping the body erect, for about 50 times, in the morning or evening, you will like it the more you do it.
9. Use of the freezing, when some one calls you, freeze, without acting it, and respond only with the minimum movement necessary, this can be used in many situations in everyday living, find more ways for yourself.
10. Stand erect, in ZERO, bend down exhaling, inhale while raising your body and hands reaching the sky, then bend again exhaling, do this for 15 times in the morning.

When you do something, do it totally aware of the now happening, focus only on what is being done by your body, with times you will master the concentration of things, and many things will become easily done, happy moment. . .

The Singing Plastique Cycle

EXERCISE	DESCRIPTION	TIMES
1. Head Turning	right to left; breathe in one side, exhale the other. . .	26
2. Head Circles	starting with head on chest, first turn one half circle up to left while inhaling—exhale down. . .then opposite direction. . .	26 ea. way
3. Shoulder Lifts Shoulder Rolls	first lift shoulders straight up to ears. . .then roll around. . .	26 both
4. Right & Left	allowing elbow to lead from side to center of body, swing arm up and around to side. . .first l., then r., then both. . .	26 for each 3
5. Wrist Shake	first shake vertically with arms bent at elbows; then shake arms outstretched with random movement. . .	26 for each
6. Trunk	first from side to side; then forwards and backwards; then in circle.	25 for all 3
7. Pelvis	first lift each hip straight up, alternating; then Belly Dancing, i.e., swirling hips in a circle. . .	26
8. Knees	first right knee in a circle; then left; then both. . .	26
9. Kicking	first right leg to right, same with left; then each leg forward and backward; then synchronize/harmonize arms going in opposite direction of the leg you're swinging forward and back. . .	26
10. S-h-a-k-i-n-g	develop a gradual increase from slow to rapid to slow of shaking whole body; legs, feet, arms, torso, ALL. . .	Enough
11. Whirling	stand centered, turn from Down Town to right, allowing arms to follow, then left, right, etc. adding energy each time. . . until you can spin once, twice, thrice to five times. . .come to rest.	

Language of the Thinking Body

The following terms, names, words, and expressions are the result of our work, while in sessions, its goal is to condense the verbal element between teacher and student, in order to increase the communication, to a sign, a word, that have a connection with an experience, a definite one behind it, thus space, time are in harmony in the workspace.

So, use them when necessary.

I can only give what I know—not what is.

1. GENERAL TERMS

*farfelu
 vision
 focus
 climax
 fly
 imagination
 ritual
 marry
 contagion
 totality
 center
 glue
*elan
 economy
 digest
 decompose
 penetrate space
 sewing together
 rainbow sound
 think elevation
 wide zero
 dramatic moment
 mark it
 commedia style

*farmelu
traject
leader
metamorphose
color
dialogue
improvisation
geometry
crescendo
approach
communicate
attunement
timing
gravity
professor
downtown
200% effort
give space
sound massage
double parallel
plumb line
physical mantra
become it
*inner clarity

2. EXERCISES

 spiral
 withdrawal

interwinding
self-exhaustion
swallow space
pull yourself
pelvis circle
emptiness through movement
red light (freeze)
green light (go)
touch the sky
stick, thread, wind
open the body (maximum)
close the body
let yourself be pulled
* 1st. trip—stillness
* 2nd trip —realization, and isolation
*3rd. trip—body catches fire
 sit like a king
 spiral—elasticity of muscles, of thought
*ifaf
*ofaf
 warm up
 shoulder leader
 slow motion
 reach up
*immediate replacement
*expand into it
 follow the rhythm
 squeeze the space
 pierce the space
 caress the space
 steal the space
 caress your aura
*a step is done
 going to the grave
 find the animal in yourself
 make love to space
*duel in the darkness
create space
*2000 years
 group consciousness
 center axis
 field of energy
 keep the mask
 psycho-physical cycle
 line of thought
 circular siren sound
 explosion in space
*dialogue—when he speaks, you shut up
 inhale voluntarily—
 exhale involuntarily

 *immediate balance
 half movement
 transitions chevaucher
 organized anarchy

have a system
paint the space
stuttering of movement
master the situation
chopped meat sound
motion in stillness
stillness in motion
stations of the body

3. TECHNIQUE

 parallel
 wheeling
 stacatto
 isolation
 atom
 bascule
 bases
 freezing
 contagion
 masks
 skating
 horse riding
 eifeel tower
 snail cycle
 moving fixation
 the cheater
 moon walk
 push space
*Egyptian profile
*cycle plastique
*centre fixe
*wheeling walk
 horse walk
 stick work
 emptying movement
*chevaucher
*echo
 tripping
*pendulum
 contrepoid
 ramasser
 leaders
 lightning
 puppets
 bicycle
 tightrope
 snairl way
 rope pulling
 voice gravity
*base fixe
 detached bascule
 figure skating
 British flag
 the cat

90

paradox enchainee
slow motion
swallow space
threefold position
emptying words
bascule walk

*ceremonial walks
 back twists
 animal work
 spine twist
parallels wall
        rope
        ladder
        stairs
        pushing
        pulling
 study darkness
 body distortions
 tree blowing
 squat knee exchange
 walk in sand
 squeezing egg walk
*undulation (sea horse)
 steal the space
 caress th space
 seduce the space
 balance (one foot)
 walk like a king (queen)
 the knife (flat parallel hand)
hands; ball
        beggar
        indication
        violin
        oriental
        flat
        the beautiful
        fist
        so what
        OK

 the bird
 tapping cycle
 the unexpected
 the drunk
 stick combat

 the boat
 pelvis drop
 running on the place
 walking on the place
 walking against the wind
 pelvic circle horizontal

lines in space
relaxed swinging turns
shake whole body
rhythmical breathing walk
crescendo mantra movement
body explosion (recycle energy)
explore the space—
passage between the vertical line to the horizontal line

4. BODY CONSCIOUSNESS

 actualize
 zero
 body listens
 thinking body
 fixed attitude
*double pin
*mercury movement
 slow, slow motion
 rooted to the sky
 rooted to the earth
 do it with a relaxed body
 move for the sake of moving
 kiss with your elbow
 hear with your eye
 say it with your shoulder
 ask the question with your whole body
*presence
*flechi
 tail clay
 whole foot
 duck consciousness
 soap consciousness
 brush the space
*fluidity of movement
 let your body work
 see with your pelvis
 listen with your whole body
 listen to your friend's knee
 smell with your eyes
 swallow with your nose
 body first—hands and face last
*walk on your head

elan turn ½ ¼
turn around center axis
body as clay—wire—stone—wood

passing and carrying the weight
rock on feet
(heel to toe)

91

holy workspace
● **the centre of silence** ● jump
into yourself ● symphony of being ●
mind-body harmony ● essence of yourself ● dot in
space ● drop in the sea ● think movement ● still as a
mountain ● a l'italienne ● the body cannot lie ● slower than
that ● timing the space ● spacing the time ● blah blah blah ● the
tragedy of focus ● you are the text ● joke number 36½ ● **burn, but
not to ashes** ● suicide, but don't die ● swim but don't drown ● listen to
your body ● **thank you for being here** ● center yourself ● **from ecstacy to
lunch** ● **the one who** ● relax in it ● unarchy ● freak in ● everyday movement
● 2 stones get stoned ● find your axe ● line of work ● **alert like a cat** ● **claying
around** ● out of it ● **be your own mirror** ● sharpen your sword ● **send a telegram** ● **perfection in action** ● brick by brick ● build a mold ● measure your energy ● **verbal fast** ● **day of silence** ● fingers of the feet ● jump into the fire ● go
mad with it ● be sincere with it ● such mastery! ● **be a whole in the detail and
the detail in the whole** ● always come back to zero ● it was not projected ● no
leader, no follower ● don't panic ● **the genesis of the self** ● one breath class ●
thought to action ● no philosophy ● do the unexpected ● no mediocre
movement ● do not manipulate ● moving mandala ● digest the food ● take
a picture ● be sincere with it ● instrument ● it must project ● be with
yourself here ● the body as a brush ● a pinpoint of light ● **to be and
not to be** ● tubes of vision ● tubes of communication ● dancing
diaphragm ● a circle inside itself ● **echo of a whisper** ● crys-
tallized thought ● **serve the idea** ● it can be seen ● be
true to yourself ● penetrate space ● explore the
space ● cut through space ● don't rape the
space ● it is known ● **you are
unique** ● names
are cloaks ●
think with your body ● **organized
panic** ● confront the situation ● move into
space ● challenge yourself ● try not to try ● don't
act it ● what is, is ● silent acting ● stand still and be ● attention not tension ● **shower on fire** ● mark each new thought
● dancing dots ● think child ● psychic surgery ● immediate reflection ● moo like a cow ● see as for the first time ● **turn the negative to
positive** ● do you have a passport ● do you have your balls ● the marriage of Mr. and Mrs. Lips ● don't be too nice with yourself ● let your body
teach you the movement ● **application is a dear time** ● are you leading the
movement or is the movement leading you? ● **the leader of a group must be
hidden** ● the circle is everywhere ● **a relaxed hand is the most beautiful** ● **what
is learned must be digested** ● mime taught me how to live ● the workshop is
not here ● your pelvis is in outer space ● we are after the essence and the essence is after us ● **laboratory of the self** ● jump in and swim into it ● **awareness
prevents accidents** ● write the text with your body ● you don't make love, it
makes you ● we have only this one body ● **not revolution, evolution** ● a mime
must know his spine, vertebrae by vertebrae ● whatever your understanding
● we can tell a person's progress by his control of the eyes ● nothing would
exist without parallels ● it is not to make people laugh ● **a circular
movement is the most pleasing** ● **the worker is hidden in the workspace** ● give it the proper amount of energy ● show the little un-
awarenesses of Man ● get in a group and work individually ●
performer, performing, performance are one ● dialogue
with the earth ● we are not in prison here ● put
your consciousness to the part of the body
you are working ● don't be any-
one but yourself

92

● no unnecces-
sary movement ● **point of depar-**
ture, center of return ● never be angry
with your body ● take the class with you ● take the
movement to its limit ● take a picture of yourself in the
attitude ● the process here is one of absorption ● try to see
things said simply ● know how to be in the other person's space ●
does your hand shape the objects or the objects shape your hand? ● it
is not to be a magician of the stick but to see what the stick can teach us
● write the exercise with your body ● if you want the space for you, you
should give it to another first ● the drunk can teach us a lot about life ● do
the illogical, the unexpected for a laugh ● **relaxation—a conscious readiness**
to respond ● let your breathing lead you ● find the animal in you ● **is the**
movement doing you? ● be true to the action ● let the movement be seen ● **we**
are cells in the body ● **we are in the process of refining the instrument** ● go
mad with it—become what you are doing ● put your energy in the center ●
prostitution of the art form ● leave words behind when you come into this
space ● it is time to be with yourself—nothing would exist without the circle ●
the dot that is yourself ● **don't do it, let it be done to you** ● **the magician of**
space ● **everything is connected** ● motion in neutrality ● be imperialist ●
embrace the opposites ● expect the unexpected ● forget about technique
● **edge of gravity** ● **grasp the void** ● stuttering of movement ● **poet of**
space—P.O.S. ● stuttering of the eyes ● **voyage pour l'inconnu** ●
don't anticipate ● dog breathing ● motion, not emotion ●
enjoy the process ● state of mind ● let go ● transcend
yourself ● **rewind the film** ● see yourself doing it ●
be here ● pour yourself ● **posture of**
openness ● hiss like a snake ●
humm like a bee
● **eyes into the**
horizon ● act with the body ● **col-**
lective orgasm ● **a leaf in the wind** ● sing
your death ● lubricate the joints ● squeeze an egg
● pass through death ● **curtains of silence** ● **organic**
sound ● hug the universe ● exquisite clarity ● weight 50-50 ●
75-25 ● **empty the cup** ● heels kissing ● inner work ● be with it ●
be your own mirror ● auto-suggestion ● **visualize the whole** ● **carry**
the thought ● **face the situation** ● **fantasy in space** ● **empty the words** ●
verbal labyrinth ● **speak to the point** ● it's not to go out, it's to come back
● first you become a craftsman, then artist, then a magician ● **in the midst of**
agony, there is hope ● thought plus movement equals action ● don't translate
words into movement ● you do it until it is doing you, then back to center ● in
transitions use crescendo of rhythm from one space to another ● it takes alot of
strength to be an old man ● invisibility makes sound, the void creates space ● if
you are afraid of something—do it ● pressed together like wheat ● a moving letter in space ● enter the space of a tone ● one yes remembered itself ● laboratory—process of integration, assimilation, experimentation, expansion, becoming, visualization ● see the line of your own body ● **they space out—we**
space in ● show confusion, but don't be confused ● there are many shades
between black and white ● do it like doing it to yourself ● mark each
new thought and the end of each thought ● the great fox in the night
speaks to me ● transform pressure into challenge ● keep the ex-
tremes, but stay in the center ● **a mime needs no mirror—a**
mime is the mirror ● learn to love without attachment ●
let your inner brilliance shine through ● we are not
working to make people laugh ● enthusi-
asm of the moment ● **point be-**
tween yes and no

93

● **expectations**
without theme ● work in the
possible space ● one foot chasing the other
● **be colorful with boredom** ● don't swim in the
philosophy ● **vigorously, not violently** ● **the body is a**
heavy feather ● **let the weight lead you** ● **be concerned, but**
don't worry ● **the body is a container** ● there is a dying in the laugh ●
don't be tickled by the audience ● **being faithful to the curve** ● discreet
readiness, invisible awareness ● close your eyes when you exercise ● don't
kill the experience ● psychic/spiritual body massage ● **suggestion of the**
dancing hands ● if you go too far, you restrict your movement ● if you really
follow the echo it will go into infinity ● to be aware of space is to be aware of
yourself ● it appears free, but it should have an order ● **slower than you think,**
slower than you are—it is there but it is not there ● **put the words in the bank** ●
nothing exists outside of this space ● the work of the feet is hidden ● feelings,
moods, thoughts are colors ● **be detached, but not indifferent** ● **say yes with the**
whole body ● **go with your intuition** ● do exercises with a beginner's mind ● you
are a cell in the group ● **to the point—measure your words** ● **Om—Mushkil**
Gusha—Nasrudin ● **be at peace with paradox** ● make image real through detail
● **close your eyes and be** ● thoughts are multi-dimensional parallels ● a
fixation is a prolonged freezing ● you are doing it for yourself, even if the
whole world doesn't understand ● if the eyes are moving, you are not
doing it ● holy workspace ● **the centre of silence** ● jump into yourself
● symphony of being ● mind-body harmony ● essence of
yourself ● dot in space ● drop in the sea ● think movement ●
still as a mountain ● a l'italienne ● the body cannot
lie ● slower than that ● timing the space ●
spacing the time ● blah blah blah ●
such mastery!

Students' Experiences

During time of our work, interviews with my students, and while following closely their Progress, and the Blooming of their abilities, it is proper to let them BE HEARD, with their "WORDS" to describe, and share their beautiful experience with you. This space is dedicated to those ones who showed dedication, joy, and Concern, while studying At Le Centre du Silence, in Boulder, Colorado.

You have to be your own cook in the kitchen, your own Shakespeare, your own composer.

96

I'm not here to give answers. I'm here to stimulate questions.

"My work in the UMW spanned 3 full years of mime workshops and two summers of performing/studying with BMT. To list the changes in my self during the work would be an endless task because, as the work continues where I am now, so the changes continue.

The seeds planted in that time continue to break through the earth and reach for the sun. Fundamentally there has been a basic change of perception at the core of my existence that has to do with the initial recognition, or awakening, of that within me which knows. The knowledge of this has lent a perspective to all that concerns me that is radically different from that which came before; it is, in a sense, the third point of a triangle which gave me stability.

Samuel Avital is a miniscule mad Moroccan who has had me treading on hot coals and broken glass, walking miles and never moving an inch, trying to convince my closest friends of my name, going to the grave, begging in the rain, silently screaming with non-existent pain. . . all the time either doubting my sanity or his or, during my finest moments, the sanity of the world. But somehow in the process studying with him I have accepted responsibility for my being on all levels, and that, to me, is important."

CHARLES GARDIEN, GLS

"When I began my exploration of this art form, I didn't realize that I was embarking on an evolutionary leap that went beyond my wildest imagination. Through this art I began to receive keys to doors that I had never known existed.

Suddenly everything that was done became a study in learning, a chance for perfection. Looking at something becomes a beautiful experience when you know the secret of stillness. Watching a child walk becomes a fascination when you have experienced gravity.

Mime with Samuel is more than a performing art. As he says, it is a 'multi-dimensional reality'. All aspects of living are encompassed in order to learn this 'art of being and becoming'. To study with this man takes nerves of steel, a mind of ice, and a burning desire to learn. Your desire to learn must outweigh your desire to be something wonderful.

From Samuel I never expected less than the truth and never wanted more. This, for me, is friendship in its purest sense.

The garden that provided the space for this feeling to grow in me was the Unique Mime Workspace. Samuel provided the 'elements' for growth. His is a garden well worth cultivating."

BRUCE McCLELLAND

97

"When I began my study of mime. I was a very nice person, flowing along with whatever life brought me, much like a lily pad on a quiet lake. I enjoyed life, liked people, had lots of fun—like all the 'nice' lily pads. What I didn't know then, was that there was a seed that was beginning to grow, seeking nourishment so that it could begin its development into the blossoming radiant flower still to come. Suddenly, there was a stone dropped in the water, in the form of a little man called Avital. The ripple was felt by everyone, but most saw it as just another ripple. This particular lily pad, however, was shaken to its very roots and, instead of remaining it its comfortable sphere, it was drawn to follow the ripple, and soon found itself quite transformed and in another world entirely.

Samuel has multitudes of colorful paths to showing you your own self and sharing unique ways of channeling energy and discovering new realms of being. It is an experience that can only be known through the workspace and a desire to grow into the amazing universe around us.

The experience of mime has brought to my life a whole spectrum of understanding and awareness that had been in a state of dormancy for years. I found that what I had always taken for granted as being 'empty space' was, in fact, an entire world waiting to be shaped. As we never read the space around the letter, so we never look at the space around ourselves.

And so, I discovered Mime—the beauty, the artform that is formed from the inside out, the mother who has within her all artforms, and takes care to nourish and protect the essence within her until it comes bursting forth in a spring tide of silent simplicity, reflecting all the world around her in the oneness of motion and stillness."

ILANA BEN-GAL

"How to mail a letter. Where to put the stamps. For weeks Sam kept showing me how to prepare a letter. I kept thinking this is so silly. It's just a letter.

One day I spent 6 hours typing for Sam. I numbered the pages by hand. I was sure there were no typing errors. He looked at every page. At page 14 he stopped and said, 'See this 4 (It was sloppy)—That's how you are in life'. Two years and fits of anger later, I'm still learning what perfection really means. When I'm exasperated Sam says, 'Fight, but go back to work'.

Striving for perfection in much different than reading about it, and much more fulfilling. Mime? How does one expect to give as an artist until he

can successfully live his own life? Through mime Sam teaches life."

CHRIS KANALY

"I discovered that the techniques of mime created an inner life force and developed in me an inner rhythm. . . a power that overwhelmed my body, took hold of my being and it grew from the bottom of my feet to the top of my chest—and also a coordination of grace, beauty came into all of me. . ."

STEVE WHITE

"I have found the mime workspace to be a space for studying oneself. Ideally, it provides the right place, the right time, and the right people for making this study. In the work we go from thought (which you think you understand) to an action (which shows you you don't understand) and try to learn from our mistakes. Sometimes it's fun, sometimes it's slow and painstaking and much patience is required. If we want to express, communicate, share something through mime, I think it has to come from a deep understanding of ourselves and our environment. In the workshop, we work alot more on that understanding than on mime technique. The learning is subtle, but it is permanent because it happens at the core."

LESLIE COLKET

"Mime teaches us to see the more subtle possibilities latent in human nature.

If the work is difficult, it is because we are undoing the influence of our culture which has conditioned us to think that a healthy person is only a collection of well-defined limits.

But here, we try to accept the limits in our work and relationships while remembering that within our own limitations we can find infinite space in which to grow."

LIZA CLEAVES

"I am constantly being faced with problems which require total self-honesty. Am I really tired of working? Am I really a piece of clay right now? Do I really want to do mime? Well, if you really want to do mime, Sam has the tools, so use them, exhaust them and you will find you get what you really want. But it's nothing to write about and everything to do."

ALEXANDRE LUMIERE

"Mime.
Learning the discipline of digesting silence, learning to mold every movement from hell to heart.
Hesitations.
Rumblings to a slow wordless shout.
At times tears seem close, at times I am confused, not knowing why I am in this class, and at moments, a few tenuous moments, it is clear, I am clear, and the breath pauses.
I bite silence.
The morsel fulfills."

LAURIE MORTON

"With each class I awaken to subtle and significant things about my own body and movement—its relationship to other bodies in space and the harmonious ways in which we can work together and create together."

BILL McCORMICK

"I've discovered my body. All these years I've had it and, until I started studying mime in LE CENTRE DU SILENCE in Boulder, I'd never explored its possibilities, its dimensions, its expressive potential. Reaching in toward my inner self through increasing awareness of the physical body. Realizing the center—that place of simultaneous emptiness and fullness which is clear and calm. Through discipline I am finding freedom."

L. BARAKA

"My impression of the Unique Workspace after only a few sessions is that it has something very valuable to offer to a person seeking to cure himself of insensitivity and egoism. The reason behind this is that Avital places the emphasis on understanding the human condition rather than simply learning a variety of mime techniques. There are techniques to be learned in the group interaction, buy they are picked up not by imitating, but rather by understanding what happens physically and psychologically at different moments."

BRIAN SMITH

"Studying mime is a growing joy for me. I have become so much more aware of my body and its possibilities; I surprise myself at times! My heart has opened even more to the beauties of the spirit, the love of God."

BARBARA BUSHNELL

"Since I began mime I have been amazed to discover how unconscious I am of my body movement and how much time there is between my thought and actions. Mime is a total microcosm of life for me.

ERIC SILVER

"This mime class is beginning to make me realize what it means to SEE."

MICHAEL RYAN

"Mime has done something for me that three years in a psychiatrist's care didn't do."

GAYLE SCHULTZ

"In the Mime Workspace I explore myself. I objectify experience in order that I may discover its essence. The expression of this essence is too complex—too simple for the spoken word. So, in the world of silence, my body becomes my tool and I teach it to become the expression of the experience. In Mime I learn to 'feel' the harmony between body, mind, and soul which I have always 'known'. I see the world around me and the world within me with new eyes. Through Mime I have experienced the energy within movement, and am learning to channel that energy into patterned movement. In silence I see the beginning of movement is stillness—and stillness becomes my own search for zero."

SALLYE RICHARDSON

"When I left for Boulder to join Samuel Avital's workspace, my friends asked me. "Why mime?" I replied, "It wil be a whole awareness experience". At the time those were only words. To talk about and to experience awareness are two very opposite things. I am just beginning to experience a new awareness I thought I already had. Every movement, every thought must have an awareness. I have discovered that Sam's workspace is not just a fun la-la-la game where we make faces and discipline our bodies. . . it is a very serious time for self exploration (which can be quite painful). It requires complete dedication, concentration, and integration of mind and body. . . Only after that can the essence be communicated."

KATHLEEN KARP

"For me, mime is communication with all the brains in my body, being in touch with all parts of myself, the internal space as well as the external. Doing the impossible, through awareness of my limitations, stretching the limitations and going beyond the limitations. Feeling lighter and free after having done them. Becoming aware of the flow of other peoples' energy, allowing space for their energy, adapting to it, blending and bending with it to experience a beautiful flow of hard work, play, love, harmony."

MAJA LENERT

"There is no beginning or end, there is only the silence of space which the mime must enter. A seed has been planted, it is the center from which all comes and all must return. The art of mime is more than the ability to perform a set of bodily movements, it is a discipline which originates in the essence of our being. Mime is the tool which allows us to move towards the source of communication. It is vital for the mime to become an unmoved center, reaching into space giving life to the invisible.

These are merely words for something that can only be understood beyond the realm of words and thoughts. Images are helpful, but it must be experienced and lived. I am here to experience and live it through my committment to The Mime Workspace.

FRAN SMYER

"Mime is a disciplined system of experiential awareness training in which the student learns how to discover new possibilities of expression and being within himself. Spontaneity is consistently emphasized as a desirable human attribute that may be developed, and the maximum creativity possible is encouraged in each student. Physical awareness is achieved by constant observation of self and others, with careful attention to the hidden messages that the human body can project. The physical exercises are designed to enable the student to isolate each part of the body so that liberation and freedom may be possible.

Mental processes are also tested and tested again by unique teaching situations being presented to the student and his group where non-linear thinking processes must be used in order for the student to understand what is happening to him. Emotional training is also an important feature of the mime work, and here it is that the student is given an opportunity to study his many hidden selves through the creation of unexpected situations which throw him off balance into unknown areas of experience where he can transcend himself and discover new dimensions of consciousness and being.

In summary, mime exists as an authentic vehicle for achieving self actualization of the individaul and is taught by a true esoteric Master in the Work.

This has been my own experience in mime after three weeks of training."

DON LENERT

"Here one is dealing not just with bodies, but something closer to total beings. Changes begin to occur from sources that affect one's entire being—that are total and organic, rather than superficial bodily changes (such as one might find in other movement classes).

Developing a total and precise awareness of one's being, body and, therefore (since it is through our bodies that we experience the environment), an increased awareness of oneself in space, as part of the total environment and energy.

Becoming more and more in tune with one's own rhythm and hence the rhythm of the situation as a whole."

JULIE BALTER

Mime cannot be learned from books. It is passed down from teacher to student.

"Samuel teaches mime through awareness. As I progress through each class or initiation, tremendous yet simple lessons concerning the essence of life upon this planet are realized. Total attention in each holy moment is the ideal that Samuel awakens in me. This involves, for me, attention to the vibrational rate of all beings, attention to the space that we inhabit and move through, and attention to the force of gravity which enables us to learn the lessons of the physical plane. Also I feel the need for great self-patience as the process of not yet actualizing thoughts "perfectly" into physical movement demands patience and a non-judgemental attitude. But the balm that eases all growing pains is the joy and peace that come as we find our center and return to Source joining heaven (thought) with earth (body)."

ZOE ALOWAN

"The ability to express the infinite, in a gesture, a movement, an expression; the deepness of inner feelings, felt from within the very essence; the light pouring out from every muscle and every thought; that inner knowledge of who I AM; the inner peace that rolls in like ocean waves, soaking me in bless; and the infinite quiet which comes after long hard work. . . All of these I experience in mime, with the teaching of Samuel Avital. He becomes a channel for pure light and teaches through that. Conflicts dissolve in understanding. I have experienced my Self in the experience of mime. I have seen my body from inside, and strained to make it do what I will it to do, and, shaking with strain, suddenly remembering to breathe, and calmly I attain that position with centered awareness, and there is no strain. . . I have learned to STOP at will, and from that stopping learned to GO from a different

101

space within me, where there is the control of non-control.

My first workshop taught me about my Ego, and the second taught me about my Self. I have suddenly found myself looking at my movements from someplace above my body, and smiled in the experience of me /not-me, and cried with the pain of working so hard to get the wrist to stand still, and laughed with joy of discovery of how to freeze the elbow in space. I have danced the only dance there is, and allowed the inner space to merge with the outer space, and felt unity with all. My experience in the Unique Mime Workspace has been more than unique, it has been one of the most powerful learning/growing experiences of my life."

                                        S. LION GOODMAN

Emptiness and Fullness

"It's OK to fight, but then go back to work."

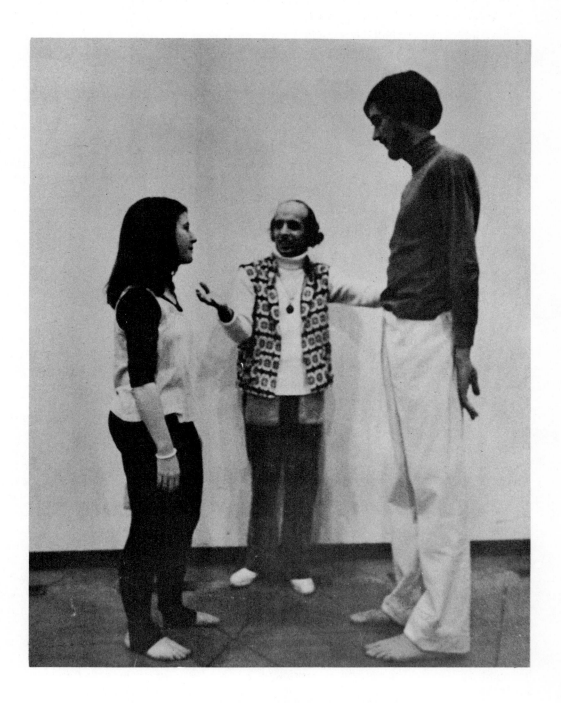

The line of your work is parallel to the line of your life.

Session of May 2, 1974 Thursday
Boulder, Colorado

OK, today we will go into the body. What is your understanding about the human body? Quite a question, you can not answer it in 5 million years, but what is your understanding as of now? Hands, lips, eyes, hair, what is it?

"A manifestation of energy."

"Condensation of a thought."

"Collection of conscious cells."

"An instrument."

"Continually changing phenomena, made of opposites, parallel lines, a dot in space."

Let's go back to the point. A dot in space, for what does it serve us?

"Container that contains liquid, gas, blood, bones, nerves, minerals, electricity, magnetism, acid, spirit, energy. It is something tangible.

"It is a whole thing, every part interrelating."

Everything interrelating, that is great, only the mystics know that. Do we know that, or do we just say it with words? How does it happen that it walks, or thinks, or feels, first think. So how is it that this matter condensed, as you say, you have a good understanding, thinks, I am asking things that we take for granted. How does it think, walk, talk, etc?

"Brain vibrations."

"Evolution."

"Life."

How do you define that word life, how does it define in you? The body is an organism of cells, organized to work on living together in spite of us. We take it for granted, not even grateful for the work that is being done. We think, act, and make mistakes, a lot is going on and we do not even know how it works.

Every cell has its own consciousness. When we become aware of the work these cells are doing silently inside of us, we begin to understand what this instrument is all about. The day you find out what your body is all about, and stay healthy, it will be very interesting. In other words, the body contains many things, not only tangible, physical things, but invisible things also. We are concerned with that a lot here when we are doing exercises from these lines. How come you have the organization to remember the line of the cycle, or how is it you can get up in the middle of the night, go into the kitchen and get a drink of water, then to back to bed as if nothing happened. You think you are doing it, but it is doing you. We will go into breathing a little tonight—even in breathing, it breathes you, it is an in and out thing. I have a story for this class, as you say the body contains things:

"There was a very wise man from Harvard University, top man, cream of the university, who went to Japan to visit the cream, top man of the university there. They sat together for a service of tea, and so Japan poured tea into a cup of his guest from Harvard. He continues to pour until the cup runneth over. He continues to pour totally calm. The other guy, the head of his university begins to get frustrated, he doesn't know what to do in that situation. Japan is pouring, and pouring, smiling all along as if nothing is happening, enjoying it. Finally the other man says, 'My friend, I know you are wise, but why do you continue to pour when the cup is full?' 'My friend you are very wise too, to notice what is happening. Because you know when the cup is full you can't fill it any more. That is your situation, you came here full, thinking you know something, but I can't fill anything into you until you empty yourself.'

So here is the point, we have to know how to empty the cup before we can fill it again. So how do we empty the cup? When we want to learn something we put ourself in a state of emptiness, a blank screen so that we can project pictures. Give me an example from your lives when you have been in such a state. If you are in that state and you learn something it is there, learned. But if you are not in that state you think you learned but you didn't really, then you become pretentious that you know. If you are in that state and learn something, you know but you think you don't know.

When there is a full cup of water you pour the water out to empty it. The pouring of water is a physical movement from up to down. You can't pour water up. We put the body in the same state but since the body there is no up and down we vibrate it into different forms. We will try to do it, it may seem silly to some of you. Start walking, what is happening when we walk. We move the body, passing the weight from one leg to the other, keeping it in motion. Keeping it in motion means vibrating in your own certain rhythm. Become aware of your body, notice things you take for granted, how your hands move, legs, what you think. Just be there for a little while. To empty your body of thoughts you have to kind of let the water gush out of you. We will try to do it with words since we think in words.

Try to pour all the words you have inside out. (garble) The mouth in this case is the mouth of the cup because we pour things through it. If the words that come out are the result of thought you're not doing it, but if the words are just words without thought, nonsense, then you are in the process of emptying. (Again everyone starts pouring out words(OK, now without words, just sounds and vowels. (Intensity increases, sounds like animals) Now we will clarify it a little just the sounds ee-aa-oo. (During the time the class is chanting they are shaking out the tensions in the individual parts of the body.)

Close your eyes, do whatever the body suggests. (The energy reaches a peak then everyone ends on the floor in exhaustion.) Relax, take your time, listen to the body, your back, legs separated, be still and listen. (bell) Listen as though you are the bell itself. See how the sound travels all over the body.

First trip is to focus on every part of the body when it is suggested. Focus on the head, no movement, just be the head, the whole body is the head. Hair, the whole container is covered with hair. Eyes, viewers of the body. All the body is eyes, see through each part. Ears, listen to every part of the body. Nose, mouth, chin, neck, be inside each of these organs. Shoulders, be with them, don't move them, they are there. Arms, elbow, lower arms, wrists, hands. Chest, waist, pelvis, thighs, knees, calfs, ankles, feet, toes, insteps. Observe from a point, your body lying as still as on water, floating dancing on the waves. Maintain stillness. Whatever image you get from the

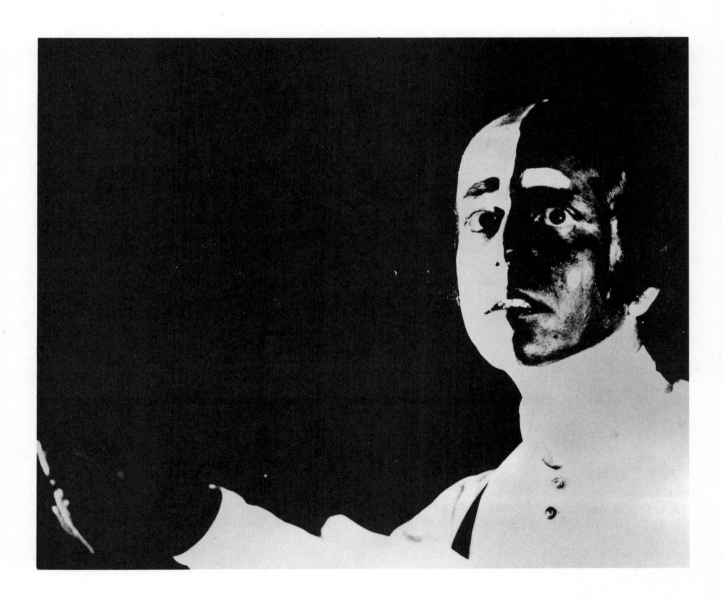

There will never be a next time. That moment passed already. You can never bring that moment to now.

105

blue sky above, become that blue, and from that blue, and focus on your self and your body lying somewhere on the planet in a place called Boulder, Colorado. Just watch it, guard it, so that it will work well, so that it will be empty, so it will achieve all desires and wishes.

While you are there see your body moving on the waves, being caressed by the waves, being carried to another dimension. The first trip is a very good thing to do when you are tired, or depressed, or wish to sleep. Listen to this voice while you are in the sky, in the blue, then when you come back you can apply it harmoniously. The other use of first trip is, when there is any disharmony in the body. Go first trip style into that part of the body, stay there, examine it, and you will be amazed when you come back out of it that, that diseased part is healed. Now come back to the body and we will go into second trip.

Second trip is the same as the first trip but you start at the toes and go to the top of your head, by yourself in silence. Make the suggestions to yourself orderly from the legs to the top. Second trip is to be born. In other words, any movement done after the suggestion of that part of the body will move accordingly as for the first time. Head, contact the area of the head, feel the neck, listen to it. Go to the shoulders, one by one, as for the first time, not taking them for granted. Arms, hands, fingers, don't move them like every day but like they have been in clay and are moving for the first time not taking them for granted, study them. Relax and just feel the sensations in the body without naming it........Silence.............

We will do the third trip next time.

Thank you for being here.
Samuel

The Boulder Mime Theatre was born out of the need to expose and present the experimental work of those who show artistic tendencies to actualize their talents in the community setting.

The sheer pleasure to share what you learn of an artistic form, in the frame of self-training, is very beneficial to the Mime students.

New areas of work are developed while guiding closely the Mime apprentice, the composition of the Mime piece , rhythm, form and content, of how to give birth to an idea, a story, while using the tools properly.

The BMT is an idea in the process of the making, the few that goes into the depths of this art form find a self-fulfilling aspect of their being, that what they know, done well artistically while their artistic personality develops and blooms.

And as part of the UMW, a branch in the tree of LE CENTRE du SILENCE, BMT serves with that public exposure to better the skill and imagination with the participation of the audience.

Repertoire changes as the members change,

choosing the material according to their learning and training and, with my direction, it is tried for the audience, and re-worked after criticism, and re-performed.

While performing in fairs, spiritual gatherings, parading on the streets, happy with another face, costumes, to a marvelous world of wonder, to share with people this beautiful art form, in Aspen, Denver, Boulder, and other places such as Lama Foundation in New Mexico, and acquiring more experience in self artistic growth, and joy of heart.

As of now we have no funds, but projects are under way to seek public donations and grants to support the work of these young and promising artists of the void, to explore farther, and have exposure to a larger public, who appreciate arts, and add to the growing popularity of Mime in America.

Some of the pictures in this section illustrate the spirit of the Boulder Mime Theatre's work.

Any idea is good. Either it turns to gold in your hands, or into ashes.

Samuel Says

"The process of mime is suppling the spine—the real spine, or the spine of understanding."

"The process here is scrubbing the mirror so you can be a clear reflection."

"We separate and work each part of the body so that later we can put them all together."

"I am interested in working with awakened people doing something with the awakening."

"I can only give you what I know—not what is."

"We are in the process here of learning to think movement. Clowns, dancers, mimes think movement."

"The dancer is danced."

"You must vibrate spiritually as well as physically."

"What is learned must be applied immediately."

"Once you have a path, there is no vacation."

"Words can lie. The body cannot lie."

"It is important to make things simple, not complex, when dealing with beings not advanced."

"The slower the breathing, the more relaxed."

"Relaxing is a push and pull of the muscles at the same time."

"We are working toward physic-physical perfection."

"Within limits, we find freedom."

"It is important to relax the parts of the body not being used in a movement."

"A relaxed hand is the most beautiful."

"People will knife you if you expose yourself too soon."

"Are you communicating or just playing?"

"Performer, performing, performance. When you master this awareness you can be called a mime, or a being."

"Achieving recognition is not the most important thing, but how you develop your life."

"If you open your suitcase too soon, it is empty."

"In mime you must create an object in a way that allows freedom of movement."

"When you show someone something you have not mastered, you are killing them."

"Stagnation occurs when you feel there are no higher levels to reach for."

"You work from where you are."

"It is important to find the center and the path to and from it."

"Nothing can harm you here."

"The development of the person is told by his control of his eyes."

"Laughter is a release from tension for the audience and the performer."

"There is no right or wrong movement, there is only movement."

"I swear to do the possible and only the possible."

"Nothing is impossible."

"Deposit the words in the bank."

"That's the work."

"We die to communicate."

"Come die with us."

"...You are in hell when you abuse words. Words can lie, but your true self, your non-verbal self cannot. Truth is what I'm after."

"Mime is more than an art,it it is a way of life. It requires a metaphysical as well as a physical awareness."

"After you are perfect, then you begin to make mistakes again."

"Freeze is a movement that takes us beyond words."

"If you are not a good photographer, the development will be unclear."

"You ride the horse. The horse rides you. You do an action. The action does you."

"Discover the theatrical aspect of ritual."

"A true artist must be in complete control of himself before presenting himself to others."

"You must live your revelations."

"Even slight movements reveal yourself."
"Be aware of the space between thought and action."

"We expand by finding our limitations and going beyond them."

"When working a piece, stay on your own level of excellence."

"Stories help us visualize the thing itself."
"Let the movemnt of the exercise remind you to feel here—not to project to another space, past or future."
"Enthusiasm is the key to crossing from a craftsman to an artist."

"If you feel the breast is dry, go."

"A teacher is one who takes what he is given and gives what cannot be taken."

"Once in the space of a piece, do not move like yourself."

"Do not be satisfied with mediocrity."

"Find your own process of learning."

"Know how to use the tools available to you."

"The first step in mime is to be understood."

"A little window in you needs to be aware of the audience."

"Mime is a visual poem."

"Mime is the art of being and self becoming."

"In the midst of confusion there must be clarity."

"Silence teaching is done in the space between the words."

"The danger is the passage from the abstract to the concrete."

"Pour yourself into the object."

"A scientist goes from the many to the one. The mystic goes from one to the many."

"See how the cosmos is breathing."

"The secret of presence is a raised torso."

"The rhythm is the blood running through you."

"An artist is like a woman."
"Not understanding personality properly, is the greatest enemy of creativity."

"The flower allows the water to go in. The flower does not make any decision to want water, it expresses the need for it. We, or Nature gives and it grows."

"Mime is not just the skill of movement of acting without words, it's process is expanding the consciousness beyond mere sensitivity."

"Jump into yourself."

"We divide in order to unite. . . not to sustain the division."

"Don't lean on each other; lean on yourself."

"If you find the process of revelation, you might cause it."

"Creation comes when you are not aware of time."

"When it is not my space, I'm not; when it is my space, I am."

"You carry yourself with you."

"The way I think I breathe. They way I breathe comes out in my movement."

"If you strive for an arrival, you will never arrive. Because there is nowhere to arrive."

"If you live on the seventh floor you can't go up without stairs."

"Mime is the presence of Creator."

"Mime is a prophet of visions."

"Be simple, but not simplistic."

"Only when you meet death, you know life."

"The beginning is the time; the end is the space."

Concentration is simply being with what you are doing.

The process here is scrubbing the mirror so you can be a clear reflection.

"When the two edges meet, there is support."

"Do not support yourself, let the center support you."

"Here we forget the everyday movement."

"Eyes open means you are asleep."

"Only when you are in the center, there is peace."

"It is not by words that energy is revealed."

"When we speak less, and breathe deeper, it happens."

"The pelvis is a plastic land."

"People imitate animals, to learn about themselves."

"A mime is a person who knows how *not* to move."

"It manifests in spite of you."

"The god of the dancer is there; the god of the mime is here."

"Orgasm is freezing."

"There is laughter, even in washing the floor with tears."

"The source of comedy is unawareness."

"Mime begins where words end."

"Simplicity is the great teacher."

"All art springs from spiritual reality."

"Mime must be earth, (bound by gravity), water, (in moving), and fire, (in rhythm)."

"It happens only in need."

"Know your limitations, and find the unlimited in them."

"Mime is an image."

"Don't lean on genius until you are one."

"If you try to form the hand, it becomes ugly; if you leave it natural, it is beautiful."

"On your table, bread and wine should be present to teach you something."

"Everything in the world is a product of condensation."
(tzimtzum)

"If the moment is constant, the future is assured."

"Be in touch with your self, so that you can be in touch with others, which are not but your self."

"We have to fight for light, because there is too much shadow."

"Male and female represent humanity."

"Before the words are uttered, the actor expresses everything."

"When you don't need a teacher anymore, you have to drop him off a cliff, or you won't grow."

"There is plenty of time, but no time to lose."

"It is not old age that stands hunched over. That is senility."

"At the point when you are ready to quit, the work begins."

"Do it, as if for the first—that is the fire that transforms a craftsman into an artist."

"When you think you can do it, your progress stops."

"To do the easy thing takes nothing."

"It is not me that is speaking—it's my experience."

"One man's sorrow is another man's joy."

"The stomach accepts everything. Fortunately the system eliminates what is not needed."

"If you want to show something, you must become that thing."

"We must forgive ourselves and others quickly, if we want to survive."

"If you verbalize about it, it doesn't happen—it's when you do it that it happens."

"You can't go to New York or Philadelphia without first going to central station."

"You get what you need."

"If you insist on needing to know why now, and you stay in that stubborness, you won't find out anything."

"They say that one who has no humor, cannot live."

"When something is finished it is finished. When you see something in the process of being finished it's much more interesting."

"A bad clown can easily be silly, sentimental, or ridiculous. But a truly great clown can create a magnificent tragicomic character, who is a one man embodiment of theatre itself."

"When a lot of people are focusing on you on the stage, it's holy. The more you give the more you are rich. God is an experience, and you cannot talk about it."

"A mime has to know to go into any space, a mime is one who when he sees 'Unknown' on a door he goes in, an average human being will fear the unknown and will stop, but the mime is beyond. We are little beings that want to go ahead."

"Now if you are going to relate to me by name or status or personality or whatever, you're not going to take anything from that criticism. But if you take that voice of criticism that comes from here as a voice from within yourself that is a very high state to be in. And that is one of the little big secrets of Learning How to Learn."

"Separation is a word that has been with me all my life. In other words, as soon as I begin to build something, as soon as I love someone, I stop doing it. It's not anythiung that I do willingly, but it's something outside of me. Part of it, because it happens a lot in my life, is that as soon as there is an achievement, there is an end. And at the end is a signal of beginning."

"Since we come to a space of understanding I will cut the word understanding and say UNDER/STAND—UNDER—UNDER—UNDER STAND. When you can put yourself UNDER, when you are able to dig a grave and disappear, when you are able to die, to raise your ego in a CERTAIN WAY—if it is a friend, if it is an idea, or anything, then you can stand. Only when you are UNDER then you can STAND. UNDER is the horizontal. STANDING is the vertical."

"Man, as artist concerned with his art, searches out the original source, the primal force, in order that he may dream and meditate, discover himself and give of himself. In both action and contemplation he is drawn to the mysterious silence. Within this silence lies the ability to know, to ex-

perience, and to communicate, herein exists the magic of Pantomime—silent music of the soul."

"Fortunately my teachers and I are different. In other words, we are different in many ways but . . .Studying with my teachers is eating some food, digesting, eliminating and that which stays is that which is you.I am not interested in that kind of student who will imitate his teacher, though Mime is imitation, and though we grow up as children by imitation, even unconsciously. But when you look into your own inner source of finding out things, then you find your way. I admire my teachers. I hate them too. But now I am in a state that is beyond love and hate. It presented itself in a certain way, that I will learn something in a certain way, so that after digestion, after the years of living and experience, you are one, you are that kind of thing. That's why in the workspace, too, I emphasize on students not to imitate me. I look for that, in other people."

"When we work movement we always ask the question who is behind that movement, I do not give it a name, when you discover yourself, you know the word God doesn't mean anything, the word religion doesn't mean anything. Mime is an art which begins to express the self when words fail."

"Everyone of us carries a certain vibration—you want it or you don't want it—you are aware of it or you're not aware of it—you carry it with you—it shows from your actions, the way you look, the way you talk, the rhythm of your walk, from the words you use, even in the spaces between your words—it shows."

"In the beginning we will imitate the animal, but after that we will have to find that keen relationship with that animal in you which corresponds to that what we call cat or dog. What is that feeling of brotherhood that you feel with that animal or group of animals? You may not have come to that—it's not the animal you like. it's the animal within. Let me tell you why I brought this up. Though only man walks and talks and all this beauty that we take for granted, all man, envelops in himself—all, all, all that is in the universe—the sound of the lion exists in man—the movement of the fish exists in man—In other words, man can do all that—he can leap, he can fly— all that animals can do, man can do too."

"I will give you my own definition of mime, as I see it after twenty years of practice. For me it becomes a multidimensional reality which transcends the communication with words that are attached to only the sense dimension that we have.

That dimension, from my experience, is compared somehow to the dream world. You cannot write with words—you can, but in 500,000 volumes—you cannot write the dream. The dream has signals and symbols that communicate that we need somehow. Unconsciously the work of mime can help to work that dimension of dreams here. In other words, once the tool is sharpened enough or once the tool has worked and experienced enough or realized enough to find out how, I, the mime will fantasize, will write, will sculpt this fantasy in space. And by doing that, you are doing an act which is called in English to perform. Since I am a cutter of words, I am going to cut this word also and say Per/form PER/form per—per—per—purr—purr—the cat purr—purr—per form PRE form— in other words, you work your ideas in a certain way and PRE—Form them."

"In the beginning was the word, BEFORE the word there was motion, vibration, movement, the source of all life."

"Shakespeare said:To be OR not to be, we say: To be AND not to be."

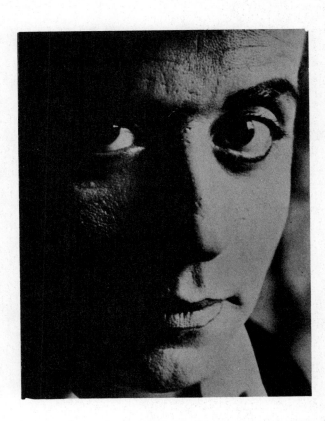

Mime in the New Age

An Interview with Samuel Avital by Ben Weaver

for the East-West Journal

Not everyone who can play the piano is a pianist, not everyone
who moves their legs is a dancer, not everyone who puts on white
face is a mime.

What happens when a five-foot tall, one-hundred pound mime—Moroccan born, Jerusalem and Paris trained—takes on an American town of 80,000 souls? In the case of Samuel Avital and Boulder, Colorado, the results seem to have been felicitous all around. The mime has found both audience and students (a class at the University, students to fill each year several three-month long workshops, and a ripening core of serious students who perform at gatherings and in the city parks under the logo of The Boulder Mime Theatre).

And for its part, the town has gained not only a serious artist and mystic in residence, but one who delights the children and adults in his performances and during the rest of the time serves as a highly visible local character, slightly outrageous in his electric blue velour trousers, black fur coat and flat-topped Andalusian sombrero. Everybody in town knows Samuel. When he performed at the University last fall the Boulder Daily Camera ran his picture—arms widespread, mouth open, eyeballs popping—eight columns wide, above the banner headline on the front page. Not bad for a man who admits, "I came to Boulder by accident."

The road from Morocco to Boulder was a long one. Samuel left his home village at age 14 and journeyed to Israel where he lived for ten years, studying physics, agronomy, religion, and living for a time on a kibbutz in the Galilee. While in Israel he chanced to see Charlie Chaplin's Limelight, and the inspiration of Chaplin's work shot him to Paris where he began studying dance and drama at the Sorbonne but soon found himself gravitating to mime and to study with Etienne Decroux.

Study led to performing, and Samuel spent most of the Sixties touring, part of the time with Maximilien Decroux's company, part of the time as a solo mime: Amsterdam, Stockholm, South America, U.S.A. A visit to New York turned into a residence there, with some teaching and performing; then a move to Dallas and a stint on the faculty of the theatre department at S.M.U. Then the final leg, three years ago—a seemingly intuitive leap from Dallas to Boulder.

We made this interview on a May morning in the living room of Samuel's Boulder apartment, which looks out onto a green lawn and the playground of the Community Free School next door. I reeled out the microphone and started the tape recorder and we sat on embroidered middle eastern floor pillows and sipped Turkish coffee and smoked his Shermans and talked.

His walls, up to about where a five foot man can reach, are plastered with photographs and memorabilia. Snapshots of his students, pictures of performances, old theatre programs and posters, a photo of Marcel Marceau, Samuel in Paris in the Sixties (hair short, very French, looking like a still from an old Truffaut film), Samuel with long hair, looking very Israeli this time, a hand-lettered quotation from Henry Miller:

> "From the little reading I have done I had observed that the men who were most in life, who were moulding life, who were life itself, ate little, slept little, owned little or nothing. . ."

And in the center of the west wall a photograph of Samuel's grandfather, the old Kabbalist, wearing Moroccan dress with a flowing white beard and a small black yarmulka on the back of his head—a beautiful, clear-eyed, serene old man's face.

The floor is covered with a Moroccan carpet, its center design of two circular mandalas surrounded by a border of repeated Moroccan script. ("You see the carpet. It says, la illaha illa 'lla' hu: There is no other reality than Reality.") I asked about his meditation practice and he showed me his meditation room—a quiet airy space furnished in the eclectic spirit of the New Age: A Buddha in one corner, a meditation cushion before the altar, and at the focal point above the altar, the heart of the Kaballah, the Hebrew alphabet.

A transcript of an interview with Samuel Avital hardly does justice to the communication that took place. For the real clinchers in his conversation are purely non-verbal: the roll of an eye, a shrug of his eloquent shoulders, a flick of a fluid hand. Words for Samuel are strictly a secondary line of communication, but here, for what they are worth, are some of the words that passed that day.

EWJ: Could you say something about the history of mime?

Avital: No mime in history has left us a clue of how he works and what were the avenues that led him to be that. We have drawings, different data, very few books but no more. Like they took the secret to the graves with them. Thus the living mime also can not say it all. It is an art that has been transmitted from teacher to pupil in a direct way. No technical books can teach mime. Thus the living mine today has to recreate his way, which is a challenge worth meeting.

It is only in this century, when Man has gone mad, that a man in Paris recreates some of the marvels of this art: Etienne Decroux who was my teacher. In times of crisis—cultural, political, so forth—those mimes, little mutes so to say, appear. In times like ours now, when the words and intellect are badly abused, then those silent beings appear to ease the madness we live in.

EWJ: Why did you choose mime as a form of expression?

AVITAL: I do mime to understand myself. There are a lot of selves I want to understand. And mime, by playing different parts and exploring different ways, becomes a channel for me of knowledge. That's all. I want to know myself. It's as simple as that.

EWJ: But why mime instead of dance or drama, which you first studied?

AVITAL: So when you are young and explore certain ways sincerely and honestly what you want to do, you explore different spheres and you don't feel at ease. So I went to movement and when I found dancing I said, "Well, I don't want to go to the sky, I want to be here." So I began to act without words. And little by little, when you are really tuned in to what you really want or what you are going to be, it shows the way to you. So you find a form. And I have found a form that is formless.

EWJ: And wordless too!

AVITAL: I will tell you the story my grandfather told me about words. When we are born we are given a bank of words. And all the words we are supposed to say in this life are there. Like writing a check of words, that's what we are doing—using that energy. If you talk too much you might finish your quota, or your account. And then suddenly you find yourself mute. And then you want to express yourself with words like everyone and you can't. This is just a story that influenced me a lot. I keep repeating it. It's my mantra.

EWJ: What is the difference between your work and the work of Charlie Chaplin?

AVITAL: Well, first of all Charlie Chaplin is a symbol for me. A symbol of a human being who realized himself in many dimensions. Though I never saw all of Charlie Cahplin's early movies, what I saw I kind of identified with a lot. Similar experiences that maybe for Chaplin and me—maybe that's what makes me identify with

him. I admire him. I think that Chaplin is a great mime. But really you can not say about Chaplin anything. That's the beauty. If you want to point out, "He is that. . ." "No, no, he is that too." "He is a director." "No, he is a musician too." "He's a great musician." "He's a dancer." (Oh, yes, he's a great dancer—greater than Nureyev. Sure, for that time.) Mime. Whew!

The great theoretician and philosopher for mime in our time is Decroux. But Chaplin doesn't need the technique of Decroux or the technique of God either. He *is* the technique, you know. He realized himself in many ways. He used his environment as it was. He fulfilled a part in history. Not only in the history of theatre or art, but of life itself. Of the whole generation that's still going on.

The mime has his own secret. Mime is an enigma that walks among us. So those people who are interested in mime really, for me, are very special kind of human beings today. Because I believe they are incarnations of great spirits. That's my belief.

In the midst of agony there should be introduced a hope.

EWJ: But how is Chaplin a mime if he was dealing with objects?

AVITAL: It doesn't matter. Mime does not mean you shouldn't deal with objects. Mime does not mean that you shouldn't use music. If you are really concerned with essence, you can use everything you want in a certain proportion. The idea is, to the mime, he has everything with him. He recreates the maya, the illusion. The mime is a mirror, a reflector. So he reflects of what you are. Even if you perform naked. Decroux, in the beginning, performed just with a slip in Paris in the Thirties. They thought he was crazy. Why? Because he says, "I am beautiful. See how my muscles work."

EWJ: Chaplin is best remembered as "the little tramp." Who is the person you present in your mimes?

AVITAL: I am presenting the man, unaware of his life, in the process of becoming aware of himself. The man entrapped in the labyrinth of living, slave to symbols, away from his center, struggling to reach that center, to be whole, integrated. When in my show I present the image of people taking drugs, I reflect—and they laugh. Then the man who is learning yoga from a book, tries to do physical exercises and has pain in his body, because he is unaware, or because of the craze of fashionable trends.

Or the man lost in the desert of technology, a robot who does what is being told without having realized his dignity of being human, or being in touch with his center. This is the image I am reflecting, because I live in it—in an epoch of transition and expansion of consciousness. I mirror the soul of my creator on stage. When I perform, it is my time to pray, to recite the poem of creation with this body-container, with the cells dancing in me, with the rhythm of the universe within.

EWJ: How has your cultural background influenced your approach to mime?

AVITAL: I grew up in a village surrounded by mountains, with a lot of waters, torrents of waters all around. Beautiful outside, but the living conditions were kind of slums Americans would never even dream to eee. You have here big apartments that are very dirty but this is not that. Narrow streets. Very little physical gratification, very little of the material element.

But when the material element is poor the spiritual element is strong. Fortunately, before birth I applied to be born into that family because in that family there was some knowledge that I aspired to. That knowledge of all knowledge, and that is the Kaballah.

EWJ: Could you say something about the Kaballah?

AVITAL: The Kaballah is a way of life. Only today, the terminology is not known. Of course it's known in books—you can be a scholar in Kaballah, you know what I mean? You can learn about terminology, you can learn about different states of consciousness there, but Kaballah deals with the experience. In other words, you need a teacher for that. It's a living form. It's a teaching of a way of thinking that allows you to expand and discover other states of consciousness that permit you to express yourself; to express that inner Self.

My early toys in childhood were not cars and guns. My early toys were this Hebrew alphabet that you see; to meditate on every letter and see what every letter really means; and what's happening when two letters come together, or three, and form a word to express a certain thing.

EWJ: Who was your teacher in Kaballah?

AVITAL: My grandfather. I remember when I was studying the prophets, and I would be puzzled by certain things that the prophets were saying, for instance Exekiel, and I would go to my grandfather quite puzzled by something that he said, and my grandfather would say, "Oh, you already got to that question?" "That's not the time to know it now." "You just go ahead."

And then some other time I'll come with a question that I don't know what is about and he'd say, "Are you sure that you don't know?" I say, "Well, right now I don't know." He says, "Well, if you think a little bit, you see that you know." And he says, "You come and ask me always questions and I know you know, but you need just to go into it a little bit, dig into it, that's all; to experience more life, more things, that's all."

In other words, it's an attitude that your teacher doesn't tell you that you don't know. Many techniques of teachers will spread around the students that they do not know. And that sits in the consciousness of the student—that he doesn't know. And he has to strive to know. But when a teacher say, "Come—you know," he instills the grain or seed of confidence that whatever revelation comes, or intuitive insight, it encourages you to study more. It's another kind of gentle way of approach.

EWJ: So he helped you to realize what you in fact really did already know.

AVITAL: In fact what I did already know. I rejected that. I didn't want to accept it because, you know, an old man, telling me that I know. And I didn't realize that he was actually transferring psychically that what he knows. What he knows I know, since we are one. Do you see that kind of relationship? Actually, psychically, he was transmitting into me a lot of things. Still.

The Kaballah training. I didn't go pay for workshop on Kaballah to learn Kaballah. As it is in this country. I grew up with it. It's my living. I understand life through that, since the Kaballah is a cosmic understanding of all that is and that is not. So it helps the understanding of the artist. And it gives me many insights of how to teach different kinds of people. Because everybody who comes to study with me, I think: "He knows." And I am there just to remind him, that's all.

EWJ: Could you elaborate on how the mime observes the world?

AVITAL: I mentioned once that the mime is a space explorer. A mime is an inner space explorer. Therefore he has to be an observer; or the observer in him has to observe many things. To classify them in a certain intelligent way, to use his total ability, so that when he begins to write with his body the expression is clear. Not the writer of a menu. The mime is the poet of space. The mime is the poet of light. Sure, this is the ideal in me talking. This is the ideal I aspire to.

Another mime might not have those ideals and would say to me, "stop with those philosophies. Perform something good." Okay. But I happen also to be a philosopher. I happen also to be a writer, a designer, an agronomer. We know this knowledge all exists here. But when you focus on one thing that you want to learn in life it will teach you everything. Even sweeping the streets of New York. You become an expert in sweeping the streets. All the companies will hire you if you will do it perfect.

EWJ: How did you happen to come to Boulder?

AVITAL: I came by accident. I came by accident to the United States. For a few months—then I stayed. I think I am where I am needed. I want to be useful to some people around me, that's all. The rest is literature.

EWJ: Do you have any plans to write?

AVITAL: Somewhere in my inner time and space I am working on a book, maybe to be called *The Process of Becoming*. To explore those ideas and those thoughts and those trainings and those realizations that brought me to like myself or to do what I do. I think it will contribute something to someone. Even to one person that would be enough. Just in sharing experience. I don't know if I am eloquent with words—I dont' know. But in silence for sure I am eloquent.

EWJ: That's for sure!

AVITAL: I don't think I am pretending anything. I like what I do and if I am eloquent that means I get through. I go to the other space of the other human being and say without words, "Look what's happening!" But amazingly speaking, when you show what's happening, you cause laughter. When you cause laughter, you release the diaphragm. When you release the diaphragm, at that moment you learn.

I am still in the exploration of why people laugh and cry. So to switch while performing a whole group of people assembled in one space from cry to laughter, from surprise to wonder, I think I am creating something in the consciousness of people to know that we are great. To know that we are more than we are.

EWJ: For me, the beautiful thing about learning to see movement is that in every moment we are making such an eloquent statement of where we are, really—not where we think we are, or say we are.

AVITAL: That's the thing. When you move truly, you live from your heart. There are people who live just from the mind. Okay. But I think in this age we are interested to live in a total way. For the line from the mind to the heart to be united; to have a wire of communication from the heart to mind, that's fantastic. That's what the kundalini is about.

EWJ: How do you see mime contributing to the spiritual movement in America today?

AVITAL: Take for instance the Sufi Choir. These people were working with Sam Lewis. They were dedicated and suddenly they have a Sufi Choir. An art form. Music. They sell records. People listen to it and dance to it. Take a Zen center somewhere in Rochester or California. They produce incense. It's an artistic thing. They produce leather work and it comes to you and you wear it and you know it is from there.

Performers of the New Age are the mimes—not Broadway or Hollywood. And mime can contribute in many spiritual gatherings that I see coming all over the country. By spiritual gatherings I mean some place where people are together and doing something with that togetherness. Not fooling around like in Woodstock. So doing something with that togetherness is a contribution. There are a few

mimes working today and we need time to train and ripen these beings, these mutes.

Many people ask me if I am doing yoga and I say that mime is my form of yoga. And they say, "No, you should take the Arica training." When you know the truth you want the whole world to go through that. But when you know a little more you begin to respect the way that your friend is going to do that. Even if he stays on his head 24 hours a day and doesn't eat, you shouldn't criticize. That's his way. We are not going to make the mistake again of the old organizational religions to hate each other because of theological misunderstandings.

Today we understand each other as artists, as mimes, yogis, Sufis, whatever. From the point of a center, from the center of a circle' you can meet everywhere as long as you don't make a barrier of the circle. And since all the streams lead to the ocean, we are there.

EWJ: Thank you very much.

We are working toward truth of expression.

130

Interview With Samuel Avital

by Annette Lust, author of:
From the Greek Mimes to Marcel Marceau

I had both love and hate for my masters; there is pain in learning through experience. We call that "pain"—when you transcent IT it is no more, and you are you. I studied with Decroux, Marceau, and others in Paris, and this was an excellent-painful-pleasure time in my life. I knew I was in the process of learning, (still am) and I bend, bow to what was given to me according to my capacities of eating, and the ability of my "stomach" to digest, and I gratefully ate with grand appetite. Thus, my style today is the result of the work done devotionally all the time.

131

Q. Why did you eventually choose mime as a form of expression rather than, for example, dramatic art which was your first theatrical activity?

Avital: To say the truth, MIME chooses me, we both choose each other; due to Theatre-Dance activity in Israel and other places, I have found movement to be my vessel of expression; due to different experiences in my life, while people were talking without saying the essence of IT; due to the noise of our time, and to seeing actors SPEAK and not ACT, I retired to the realm of silence, MIME, with training the instrument-body so that a symphony of being can be played.

Q. What is the role of mime in regular theatre? In dance?

Avital: MIME is the root, the essence of theatre—the word actor comes from the verb—to act. Every actor who is dedicated to his work must have an elaborate training in MIME in order to be complete in his total expression. It is not merely imitation and gesticulation; we all (including Dancers) work with this body-instrument, and we must learn the ways of each stream.

Q. You are both mime and a pantomime actor according to drama critics. How do you distinguish between these two terms?

Avital: Let the drama critics call me, or label me whatever they wish—the truth is one—MIME is an art form communicating the essence of life in silence with harmony of body and mind. It's an art form of becoming; that is why a Mime becomes a butterfly while working, or any object he is touching. Man created symbols, words, signs in order to communicate. If the drama critic swims in the confusion of dividing, I, the Mime artist, unite IT again—so let the drama critics play with WORDS. In my opinion there are no mime critics. The viewer sees the experience, or experiences it, and then reports it with words, symbols to be printed—he is not a critic, he's a reporter. How on earth can you give words to an experience? The language of an experience is the experience itself; words can help express your experience, but that is not all.

Q. Your use of Mime as human satire calls to mind the mime of the ancient Greeks and Romans. Do you use satire as a means of educating the spectator itself as well as an artistic means?

Avital: Using MIME as satire, comedy or tragedy—it is still an important tool of communicating that experience which is a result of life experiences, our personalities, the pettiness of our kind and the unawareness of man in the pro-

cess of destroying his self. All these are better expressed with that saitre, and to reflect our image in silence is much more effective than o do it with words. Mime unites in IT all forms of acting— —satire, comedy, tragedy, etc., and points out ways to be whole—harmonious. An educational tool? Yes, it can embrace the heart of everything. Using this cosmic language as an art form can teach many truths—ways of being one with oneself. As the Greeks and Romans did, we of this time, adapt that way to our environment, and as artist-Mimes we reflect THAT like a mirror and it serves as a stimulus for self awakening.

Q. Mime seems to be a form of religion or philosophy for you. Could you elaborate on this?

Avital: When you discover what your life work is going to be you swim into it. Mime teaches me to live harmoniously; religion means a way to be, so Mime has become for me a form of being at peace with myself. Due also to the mystical upbringing in my childhood, and my journeys in this world, Mime encourages me and forces me to go deeper into myself—to express my essence in this

When we reflect others, we reflect ourselves.

art form to people. That reflection of me into you, you into me, is the unity of communication, and above all in silence. Filling the space-silence with human feeling-colors of the painting; Mime is painting into space—I am the brush, the violin, the word, the form of condensation of the cell in the body form, to unite with other dots in the space which is none other than me reflecting IT.

Q. Mime, for you, is also a means of personal growth for the individual. Could you elaborate on this?

Avital: Sure, that also embraces the question of growth. Mime can teach awareness, sensitivity, harmony in movement and self balance of muscle and breath, soft-flesh and hard-bone. I have introduced this training to Growth Centers in this country, and actually in my school in Boulder, Colorado. Whenever I go to perform, or lead workshops on Mime, the beautiful possibilities of what Mime has to offer on this line of self-growth, self realization etc., are presented.

Q. You believe that words are a limiting factor in communication. How so?

Avital: Let me say first that I do not have anything against words—it is about the abuse that I am concerned. Speech is an energy, and it must be channeled like electricity in wires—it is limiting like any other means of communication if it is abused. Every art form is limited in a way, but in that limitation, when we expand into it, we find the unlimited.

Let me tell you a story that probably was a catalyst in my life—you know, stories convey many doors of opening more to see and experience; they elevate our level of consciousness to the heights—if you allow it. My grandfather, sage and Kabbalist, used to tell me many stories—one of them was this: When we are born, we are being given a certain amount of words to USE in our lifetime, and so we have to WEIGH what, and how we are going to use them. Any words that are used are counted, and we must be careful not to finish them early in our lifetime—otherwise we wake one morning and we find that we havefinished our quota, and become mute—no more words in our bank.

So this teaches that speech is an important energy to USE not ABUSE (as the case in our time). I grew up by being careful of what I say in order not to face the situation of having no more words at my disposal, and so MIME HAS presented itself to me—speaking less and doing more.

So I say—words—USE them only when necessary, and in their use go to the root of it—to the essence of what you want to say, and not just blah! blah! blah! Words are just symbols of the essence to recognize and distinguish between things in order to communicate only. Take for example the word "water"—it symbolizes that living-flowing-liquid that gives life in the desert; if you shout "water" a million times, your thirst will not be quenched until you have that essence called water, and only the individual himself can KNOW when they are USED or ABUSED; I love words too.

Q.You are a "street mime on stage" in that you bring characters from the street to the stage, rather than characters to the spectator in the street. Could you comment on this?

Avital: Yes, I bring into the stage (altar) the reflection of man on the street, and also man, his life and dreams everywhere; there are Mimes who go on the street to reflect that, both are valuable according to the motive of doing IT. A theatre hall is a house, the audience comes as a guest, I serve them with a reflection of themselves. They eat in silence, laugh, cry, etc., that is a fantastic process of learning, so after eating an apple, that apple becomes me. The communication between Mime and audience is focused in one space, and not scattered in the confused street. Let me bring the confused street to show IT to an assemblage of people we call audience; Mime needs focused attention—a stillness in motion that can be given an independent space in the house of theatre.

Q.Could you differentiate (or compare) between your mime expression or style and that of (a) Decroux (pure abstract mime) (b) Barrault (total theatre) and (c) Marceau (continuation of the Debureau tradition plus modern mime), not as the so-called French School but as individuals each using a very different expression. Could you also differentiate between your style and that of other well-known mimes?

Avital: Your question of comparing my work at this time in my life with my former masters is intriguing, but I will try to face it, in my way. When you study with someone who knows his field, you are hungry, you eat, you are full, it's yours—it's in you, it becomes you. With the infinite experiences in life it takes your own form, shape of your thinking—you allowed the change to happen in you, one spark absorbs the other, like two cells becoming one. This analogy of eating-learning, a separate thing becomes one, digesting, and becoming is to make clear what I say.

I had both love and hate for my masters; there is pain in learning through experience. We call that "pain"—when you transcend IT it is no more, and you are you. I studied with Decroux, Marceau, and others in Paris, and this was an excellent-painful-pleasure time in my life. I knew I was in the process of learning, (still am) and I bend, bow to what was given to me according to my capacities of eating, and the ability of my "stomach" to digest, and I gratefully ate with grand appetite. Thus, my style today is the result of the work done devotionally all the time. I am presenting the man, unaware of his life, in the process of becoming aware of himself; the man entrapped in the labyrinth of living, slave to symbols, away from his center, struggling to reach that center, to be whole, integrated; when in my show I present the image of people taking drugs, I reflect, and they laugh—then the man who is learning Yoga from a book, tries to do physical exercises and has pain in his body, because he is unaware, or because of the craze of fashionable trends—or the man lost in the desert of technology, a robot who does what is being told without having realized his dignity of being human, or being in touch with his center. . . That is the image I am reflecting, because I live in it—in an epoch of transition and expansion of consciousness, I mirror the soul of my Creator on stage——when I perform, it is my time to pray, to recite the poem of creation with this body-container, with the cells dancing in me, with the rhythm of the universe within.

I may say that I unite all styles of my teachers, blending my caractere, and experience in life, but it is me that is doing it; after preparing a dish, you

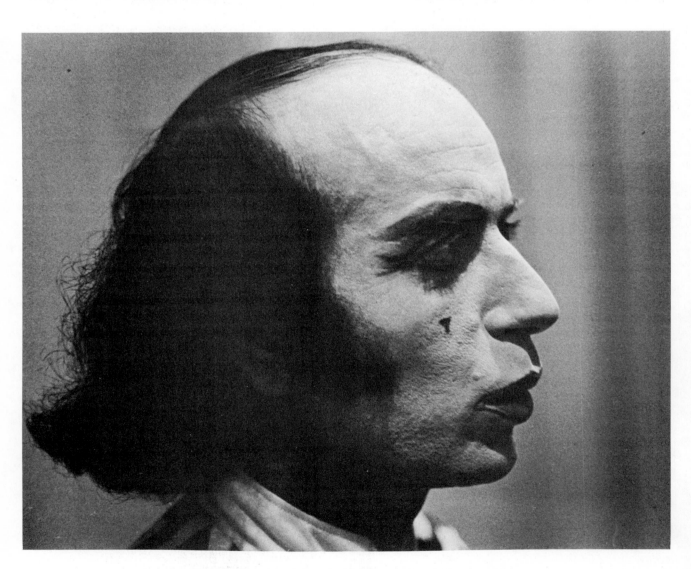

"The Mime Actor must have in his head the material of a Novelist, and in his body the muscles of a Gymnast, and above all an ideal in his heart."

ETIENNE DECROUX

eat it, it's you, with your own flavor—and it is tasty.

The difference that can be made between Marceau and me is in the experience in life that Marceau has and I have not, or that I have and he has not, so we use the same medium, with another form, another word. If one writes about his love experience, it will be different from the other writer; for the same reason, love is one, but we experience IT differently according to the total events of life at that moment—we are different, yet we are the same. I represent another aspect of being than Marceau, yet it is the same. Mime is the art of UNITING, by dividing in order again to unite etc., etc., etc.

Q. Has the American public a better appreciation for mime today than in the past?

Avital: According to my voyages here, and the audiences encountered—yes. For a few years I have been living in this physical space called America, and am grateful to it in many ways, especially to the beautiful vast audiences—

—children and adults of this country.

I find the responsive ability here very significant in the sense of willing to see new forms, and rediscover again this beautiful old-new art form—Mime—and its infinite possibilities to teach us in a humorous way to laugh at ourselves, and to learn how simple it is to be happy.

There are very few Mimes, not only in America, but in the world today, and each is working according to his or her understanding—if the audience sees different aspects of this, they will come more and more to enjoy and learn, so every Mime must be very good at what he or she is doing—not only technically, but also cosmically.

Mime is the cosmic language; it is a business for life; it never ends—it is constantly aware of the change that is happening. A total observation of the surroundings, of your self, makes the Mime a better instrument, or vessel to realize and to release the cosmic energy to others with love and devotion, so that we live in a harmonious world, so that we may know who we are really.

The Mime Experience

"The Mime Actor must have in his head the material of a Novelist, and in his body the muscles of a Gymnast, and above all an ideal in his heart."
                                        Etienne Decroux (1)

To fulfill and to realize these three suggestions quoted above for the attainment of the high quality mime artist probably will take a few lifetimes, however those who are of a keen spirit and genuinely attracted to this art should strive to at least aim at this highly profound perfection by dedicating all their energies—and put them at work without limitation of time and space.

It is not by accident that we witness in America today the rise and interest of this old-new art form, Mime, generated by the life work of a man, a teacher, and guide, Etienne Decroux. However, in a world gone mad, in our time when the word is badly abused, it is only natural, for some young people to be attracted to a silent art, that when it is done well, can be more eloquent than the word. An art that turns one to the essence of the self, of being, to discover an art, that gives them the total integration in life, and genuine artistic self-expression.

Since my first encounter with Mime and Etienne Decroux, and Maximilien Decroux in Paris of 1958, and as a practicing mime—as a way of life and living, I would like to pour out some of the thoughts, and results of experience, in order to share this with those who are really interested, in undertaking this work.

MIME IN AMERICA

While living in this country, since 1964, I have come to see, especially these days, that Mime is becoming "A la Mode" a kind of a fad. Even dancers are calling themselves Mimes, without the least profound knowledge of this art. It is an absurd situation. Not every white face in a town square gesticulating hopelessly is a mime; not by wearing a clown costume, one is a clown; not by playing a piano tune, one is a musician, not by one brush stroke on a white paper, one becomes a painter. This is the reality I witness, in my experience as Mime performer, teacher, and a concerned human being. This might lead to a sad tone. The concerned real student of mime, however can with dedication, devotion (that he or she invests in the study of mime without limiting the self to time or space) come to a realization of being and becoming an artist of great value. In his interview with Tomas Leabhart (2) Mr. Decroux emphasizes this. "Right now mime is a fad. Should I rejoice? It's a question of what one is doing with his art. Mime can be very bad. One can very well use one's body to perform like a monkey. And that's just what happens without an analytic study. You can't become a mime artist just by keeping your mouth shut. That would be too easy. If that were the case you could put mutes on the stage and say: "Perform! Since you don't know how to speak, you must know how to move!" Agitated movements and grimaces with the body won't do. If the Pantomimes of other epochs made grimaces with their faces, one can imagine those of today making grimaces with their bodies, saying it's natural, it's subconscious.

"And there we are, I am really afraid of all that. There must be schools, as described by Pascal where one studies with a geometric spirit. That's what I think we need. But we're a long way away from that!"

It is well said through experience, indeed, from a man who is the source of the 20th century renaissance of this marvelous art form.

An example of this situation: I witnessed in the International Mime festival held in Summer 1974 at Viterbo College. An international assemblage of mime performers taught classes to some 200 students from all over the U.S. The students attitude was exactly as Decroux described it. Some teachers taught pulling ropes and walking on place (by the way walking on place leads to stagnation of the person—the point is to make a step with skill) and other visual techniques without the analytic study we aim for. A mime cliche, with total attachment to technique, in a very technological culture. Dancers appeared on stage, with the mime label, pretending to know about mime, but their performance showed the truth—of the lack of genuine knowledge of mime. Very few mimes showed that approach and attitude of concern about the work they have been in for many years. The mediocrity was so clear, that even some of my students became anxious of the situation, saying that some students and artists prostituted this beautiful art form. In our discussion I pointed out that the only answer to all this is a return to the self—to dedicate their time and effort more to their work, without looking for results, or publicity seeking; by that to eliminate the mediocrity in their work, and attain if there is something to attain, in time to come. But in a civilization that looks for instant happening or instant knowing without investing any work at all, a pearl is a stone, because today everyone who holds a brush in its hand is calling it to be an artist. That is the trap that kills many on their way to real knowing. Unfortunately this way of thinking or being is very popular, for the unmature

person, who wishes to grab a thing because it is a fad. It is so in many fields as it is so with mime. As the old Proverb says: "He who learns from the IMMATURE is like the man who eats unripe grapes and drinks fresh wine; he who learns from the MATURE is like the man who eats ripe grapes and drinks old wine." (3)

THE ART OF LEARNING MIME

Having touched this briefly, acknowledging in it a dis-ease, a cure must be found, and the cure must be very harsh and firm—more time to dedicate to the analytic study besides the practical exercises, done properly by a concerned mime student. I believe on this line "Many are called but, few are chosen. The student of mime is an explorer of the inner realms of the self, therefore there must not be any limit of time and space, so those mimes with the ideal in their hearts (which actually makes them chosen) will work in such a way to elevate the average level to the excellence in their work.

To perform one must know its field, very well. There is nothing bad with experimentation, as long as it is done in the laboratory, with few people. The quality of the mime student must lie in deep concern that shows through the actions, not only by mere interest: "It's a question of having students WHO WILL ALLOW THEMSELVES to be taught and that is a different story all together." (4)

While in Paris as a student of mime with Mr. Etienne Decroux, I wrote an article called "Experience d'un jeune Mime". (5) In that article I emphasized about two ways which are one to master the instrument of expression. It said, "By these personal experiences, I come to the following conclusions. The discipline of the mime should be from a strong will: he have to possess a comprehension just, and immediate to that to be expressed, and to translate it to the movement be attained by the mime student which gives the fluidity of the self to be. This should be equal to fluidity of the self to be. This should be equal to the mental mastery of self that permits it to guide the thought properly through the body expression." With other words; the space between thought and action, is the field of the mime work in the beginning. The immediate translation of an idea, or a thought, to a concrete gesture. For that the physical instrument must be willing to learn and develop itself without any restriction of time and space,. . . When the audience sees a mime perform, if it likes it, it will see other mimes, if not, it harms the way of the other mimes. Sometimes the audience is educated unconsciously to praise the mediocrity, unfortunately. The concerned real artist should work in a way to change this reality around him or her.

This deep training in Mime, is being done in schools of some mimes. In our school here in Boulder, "Le Centre Du Silence" founded in 1971 we emphasize these points in deed and thought. There is a carefully elaborated program, of training. It is first a preparation to Know the human body, through exercise, and experience—with some practices that help on the way the student, to be in the proper frame of mind, to be willing to be taught. With other words, the student must first learn how to learn. A mime, according to my standard, must transform its way of thinking first, by very elaborated constant practice. We learn to think words in this culture. A mime must think movement, vision, images, non-linearly, and this process must be given unlimited time to explore. Only when this is mastered, we begin with the analytic work. Later improvisation comes to enlarge the scope of the work. One of our practices is to fast from words one day a week, to bring this to a habit, in order to penetrate the realm of the silence. Later we shape this silence with movement, giving it a multidimensional reality.

When interviewing students about why mime?, I have such idealistic answers with words, of one's expectations. With time, when the same student faces an actualization of working out its ideals, it gives up, drops out so to say, and that is because of that attachment of the words. It is not by saying with words that "I am a mime" that one becomes mime. One has to invest the self and all its resources to learn. This is a classic cause for all fields—that only few are chosen, in the sense of choosing oneself with the actual, practical invested in a long period of sincere study. Only this according to my experience can help produce good mime artists in our perplexed world.

THE SPIRITUAL REALITY

Coming to mime from an eastern way of thinking, helps me to see clear the way of the west. Since my upbringing was spiritually rooted, in all I do or think there is a spiritual awareness. That as performer, mime, and teacher, many ways present themselves to impart that to the students that come my way.

We would like to reach higher in this art, from better to excellence. The key for that is the awakening of the spiritual reality of the student, with no attachment to dogma. It is real when in the process of becoming the student discovers theself. Only through disciplined work, one begins to

realize that aspect of inner being, and this development will lead and assist the student to rise above all mediocrity, not only in his art but also in his life. For me Mime is a way of being and becoming, and that is also the training of mime in the lines proposed in this space. Mime is more than an art, it is a way of life, it requires metaphysical as well as physical awareness. It is an extension of the life force for channeling energies into a symphony of being. Mime is not just a skill of acting without words. It is a process of expanding the consciousness beyond mere sensitivity, time and space, and communicate clearly, with artistic skill on the stage, in order to reflect the human condition in our puzzled times.

*"The perfect square has no corners;
Great talents ripen late.*

*Teaching without words and work
without doing
Are understood by very few."*

Lao Tsu

THE MIME EXPERIENCE
FOOTNOTES

1"Etienne Decroux and the French School of Mime,"by Anette Lust. *The Quarterly Journal of Speech* Vol. LVII,Oct. 1971, No. 3.
2"An Interview With Decroux", by Thomas Leabhart.*Mime Journal*, No. 1,November 1974
3 *Sayings of the Fathers*, 4:28
4 "An Interview With Decroux",by Thomas Leabhart. *Mime Journal*, No. 1,November 1974
5 "Experience d'un jeune Mime' par Samuel Avital. *Art et Dance Magazine*, edited by Jean Dorcy, Paris February 10, 1961.

Holy he or she who with eyes open can SEE and HEAR the inner
voice to absolute truth, that this ancient wisdom of the Kabbalah
can teach us, to be whole, and one with the cosmic.

Mime and Kabbalah

Along the way I have been asked to "Explain" Mime and the way it is integrated in my Kabbalistic way of life. The word I see useful to use now, at this stage of my understanding is here, for what it is.

You ask what is Mime, Kabbalah and Mime, and I answer with a question, Why do you breathe?

Mime is as old as man's knowledge, and I am aware of the ancient use in the mystery temples of Egypt, and other ancient cultures. My integration of Mime and Kabbalah, is therefore natural for my artistic growth, and it reflects itself in the teachings to my students.

Mime originated before everything, before man utters a sound, it moved, and danced the mysteries around him, in him, in the soul of the awakening to higher spheres of life, until this very moment. Many today have gotten away from that center in the arts, the arts as it is today, is profane, and commercial and does not play a central role in life. I mean overdoing for the techniques itself. The spiritual reality, which is the source of all arts, is dormant, and we need to awaken it now, by the proper approach to this ancient art.

So Kabbalah is a very old inner science known to the Hebrews, who kept and cherished it among them from teacher to student, or better say from father to son. It says the truth, in that language of codic ciphers of the Hebrew Aleph-Beith, wtich are ideogrammes enveloping in their symbology cosmic powers, and its literature can be approached after many years of inner speculations and practical experiencing the natural laws. Its spectrum is like a magestic and awesome rainbow, and reaches every aspect of life. One need to be trained properly for it, by one who knows. That is why it is important to respect every living thing here, it might give us a hint, a clue, for our inner needs, and search for the truth.

So everything in life is communicating something very profound to us, and it is up to the degree of our awakening to cipher it, and with the sharp ability to discriminate that we KNOW the way to truth, which is what the wisdom of the Kabbalah is leading us to.

So this, to be integrated in Mime, as I see it, it is my way of life, of thinking, and BEING-NOT-BEING. It comes out in my performances and the way I teach mime.

Holy he or she who with eyes open can SEE and HEAR the inner voice to absolute truth, that this ancient wisdom of the Kabbalah can teach us, to be whole, and one with the cosmic.

141

Here we forget the 'everyday' movement.

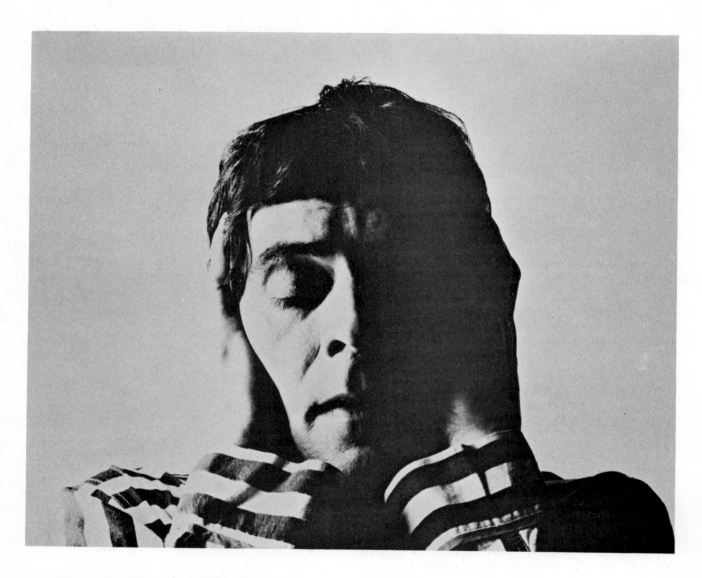

We are all, without exception, crazy.

The saving grace of Avital's craziness is that it is concerned with his own spirituality. This concern has consumed every day of his life, and however myopic it may appear to some, it is the matrix and meaning of Avital, the man and the artist.

Paul J. Curtis
Director
The American Mime Theatre

A Child and a Vision

Samuel as a baby with Parents and Brother.

A story from my childhood will be appropriate here. How a child as I was, was fascinated by first encounter with the horizon.

One day after school I found myself walking unconsciously to some unknown direction, and suddenly I realized, consciously, that I have gone far away in the fields. Looking to the horizon, under the blue skies with those majestic mountains of my birth city of Morocco on my left, and like a flute calling, I asked myself "What am I doing here? I should be home by now. My family is going to worry about it." But the landscape sight hyptonized all of my being. I stood there like a statue, immobilized with great awe, with the thought "I want to visit the horizon; I want to go to the horizon; I want to be the horizon."

And my legs walked and walked and walked. The only focal point in the horizon was a beautiful tree alone on the whole horizon line. One tree. That accelerated my fascination. And walked and walked and walked, while saying "I'm going to meet this tree. This is propbably the tree of life I have learned about in school."

The afternoon sun warmed me and I was not tired walking and just wanted to meet the horizon and rest under the tree and praise the grandeur of creation. "Oh—there—in a little while I will be in the horizon." And walked and walked and walked. The more I walked the more the horizon was far away like I was chasing an unknown form or image or idea. But when a child does something he does it whole-heartedly with all his might. And so did I.

In just a few steps I am under the tree in the horizon I saw a while ago. Well, satisfactorily speaking, I have reached the point where I wanted to go, sat under the tree and read the Psalm 104 and I understood, or pretended to understand its Kabbalistic meaning.

The blurry afternoon sky made me realize that it is sundown. Stood up and amazingly speaking I looked beyond the tree and there was another horizon. I made a few attempts to walk toward it, but I realized I have to go home backward. I turned right, left, all the sides of me, and I found the horizon embracing me, all calling me. Then I understood that in order to makeone step forward you make one step backward first. And, then while returning to my home under the stars, already the horizon becomes me, and me the horizon. Only at that zoomed moment, as a child I began to understand what is aleph. Without words. As one sage said "I wandered in pursuit of my own self. I was the traveller and I am the destination."

As of today, I'm still fascinated by the horizon. It has no beginning and no end. If you try to look at the beginning or at the end you'll never find it. And so with our work here in Boulder. Until this idea is realized by students; until it is allowed to be realized, the student will not do the work properly. Therefore, well, the horizon is you, it's in you, surrounding you like water in the ocean.

145

Samuel near Canal St. Martin, Paris, 1960.

Shemouel, by Moni Yakim

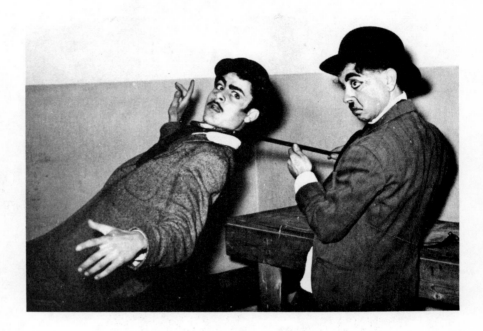

Yakim and Avital.

Occasionally, he comes out of his world of solitude, only to communicate and give the best of what he found within the depths of his soul.

I was fortunate to meet Shemouel on a such occasion.

Restless, uneducated, undisciplined, stifling with boredom in a town where most people lay in their beds at 9:00 P.M., I was an outstanding member of a teen gang.

Bursting with energy of youth, of frustration, angry, we roamed the streets, creating commotion, playing tricks that often led to minor crimes. This was my Jerusalem of 1951.

One evening, determined to take a good look at the sexy pieces in leotards, we set out to the youth center where a dance class took place. It was a disappointment. There were only two girls in the class, and they were dogs. With some not so refined gestures and sounds we started out. I suddenly was encountered by the biggest pair of

eyes I have ever seen, staring at me disapprovingly. My immediate instinct was to punch the bastard little man right between his cow eyes. But then he smiled and that was the turning point in my life.

It was a ritual. Every Friday afternoon he came to my house. After gloating on my mother's cooking, comprising mainly of rice and bean soup, we went to his "house." It was a tiny little room with a small bed, a chair and a little desk. The walls were covered with drawings of Shemouel for at that time he was also a student of painting.

This was the room in which I learned that there are things other than beating and stealing and that one can actually get his kicks just by sitting with Shemouel, listening to his words, daydreaming. He spoke of things foreign to me and gently, gradually, they became familiar: Paris, art, culture, mime. Mime above all. Mime was the

Moni Yakim, Director of Pantomime Theatre of New York.

dome under which the world is awaiting its discovery, and we shall discover it.

Enchantment, mystery, flight on the wings of strange and lofty ideas. Sensing creation, touching the Gods. This was the first chapel I have ever been in.

Consequently, I devoted more time preparing myself for the theatre and roamed less the streets. I joined classes in acting and dance and eventually we both took part in the founding of a theatre in Jerusalem.

Paris and Shemouel had to wait patiently till the completion of my long and miserable military service. Finally, the long awaited day arrived and we took the first step towards the realization of our dreams.

We were in Paris, studying with Etienne Decroux, the creator of modern Mime and with Marcel Marceau, the greatest mime performer in the world.

These were beautiful times. These were hard and trying days.

Living in a tiny room, at an old lady's apartment, our diet consisting exclusively of one can of sardines and one baguette per day—we were studying and living with mime, and we were elated. We practiced on the table, which was the largest available area in the room. It was our "stage." We took turns practicing on it.

There were discussions, there were arguments.

> There were discussions, there were
> arguments.
> Concepts began to form, ideas, opinions.
> We were developing styles, but our styles
> differed.

We were together, yet we were alone. Shemouel needed his solitude. It was means of survival to him. One thing was never in question—our love for Mime. We gave ourselves to it entirely. Years passed by.

We came to a cross-road and followed different paths. I toured Europe with Grillon's Mime Theatre (She was an old time pupil of Decroux's) and Shemouel joined Maximilien's Decroux Mime company.

Meanwhle, our dear Master, Etienne Decroux, was preparing to leave for New York, to open a Mime school there. I followed his steps about a year later to join his school and newly formed Mime company. Shemouel stayed in Paris with Maximilien's company.

A few years later Decroux decided to return to France and I have decided to open my own school and Mime company. I urged Shemouel to come and join us, which he did.

But this reunion was different from our partnership in the past. He joined the company yet he was elsewhere. He has developed his own ideas and philosophies, which I admired but which were very different from my own. Shemouel needed his solitude to make his plans, to structure tis thoughts. He needed his own flock.

Shemouel is in Boulder, Colorado now leading his Unique Mime Workspace, and I am in New York, leading my own Mime workshop and school. However we are together. Shemouel of 1951, for the better or for the worse is what I am today.

If you seek some truth or direction in life or art, stay close to Shemouel for he might just then crawl out of his shell and give you of his soul.

MONI YAKIM
Director, Pantomime Theatre
of New York
New York February 1975

Moni Yakim and Samuel on Jardin De Luxembourg, Paris, 1961.

Photo Credits

Photos By:

Cover: Robert O'Connor
Back Cover: Robert O'Connor

Robert O'Connor: p. 1, 26, 28, 36, 38, 40, 42, 48, 52, 53, 56, 60, 62, 64, 68, 69, 72, 76, 78, 80, 101, 113, 115, 116, 120, 121, 122, 123, 125, 143, 146, 147, 152
Prisme Photo: p. 149
Daniel Franck: p. 8, 18, 19, 21, 22, 23, 24, 50, 119, 130, 132, 142,
Kriss Fleury: p. 148
George Delarue: p. 5, 6, 128
Jonathan Santlofer: p. 15, 82, 105
Owen Brown: p. 74
Mehdi Khousari: p. 125
Jamie Anderson: p. 12
Doug Campbell: p. 30, 37, 46, 66
Doug Piper: p. 29, 58, 70, 134
Motherlove Barnett: p. 25
Lion Goodman: p. 33, 34
Dan Raabe: p. 165
Jerry Cleveland: p. 7, 17, 57, 108 upper, 127
Michael Klein: p. 140
Alice DuCoeur: p. 107
Brian Paila: photo of Marcel Marceau
Jerry Stowall: p. 108 lower
John Puerner: p. 109, 110, 111
Bill Ray: p. 44, 62
Kathleen Karp: p. 9, 28, 41, 73, 97, 96, 103, 118, 166
Sallye Richardson: p. 88, 102, 131
Jim Moore: photo of Paul J. Curtis 144
Mina Yakim: p. 150, 157

Appendices

Articles, Interviews, Reviews, on or by Samuel Avital

UN ART EN PLEIN ESSOR by Gabriel Roth. L'information D'Israel. Tel-Aviv, Israel. Feb. 5, 1961

EXPERIENCE D'UN JEUNE MIME by Samuel Avital. Art et Danse. Paris, France. Sept. 1961

LE MIME AVITAL NOUS PARLE DE SON ART by Jacques Bertel. Amities France Israel. Paris, France. Dec. 1961

UN JEUNE MIME ISRAELIEN REVE DE CREER LE "THEATRE DES MIMES" by J. Rabin. L'Information D'Israel. Tel-Aviv, Israel. Dec. 26, 1961

AVITAL—UN JEUNE ESPOIR by Jean Farhi. Masques et Visages. Paris, France. April, 1962

LES ECHOS DE LAS SCENE L'Information D'Israel. Tel-Aviv, Israel. Feb. 8, 1963

UNE SOIREE FRANCO-ISRAELIENNE AVEC SAMUEL AVITAL by Henry Bulawko. Amities France Israel. Paris, France. Feb. 1963

IZRAELSKI PANTOMIMISTA W PARYZN by Tuwia Karmel. Polonais "Nowiny i Kurier". Tel-Aviv, Israel. March 29, 1963

AVITAL-MIMUL ISRAELIAN, LA PARIS. Viata Noast. Tel-Aviv, Israel. April 8, 1963

EXPRESSION: LA MIME by Christian Mallet. Rencontre. Paris, France. April. 1963

SEUL LE SILENCE EST ETERNAL by Gabriel Roth. L'Information D'Israel. Tel-Aviv, Israel. Feb. 7, 1964

AVITAL, LE MIME AUX CENT VISAGES. Comparaisons. Paris, France. 1966

PANTOMIME ARTIST USES LANGUAGES OF BODY TO CONVEY ABSOLUTE TRUTH TO AUDIENCE by Vivian Witt. The Cleveland Jewish News. Feb. 3, 1967

DIALOGUE BETWEEN MIME AND SKEPTIC by Jack Anderson. Dance Magazine. New York. Aug. 1967

AVITAL: THE INSECT by Kimble Mead. The Prattler. Brooklyn, New York. March 5, 1968

AVITAL'S AIR FORMS OF PANTOMIME by Nancy Hom. The Prattler. Brooklyn, New York. March 12, 1968

THE ART OF SILENCE by Samuel Avital. Comparaisons. Paris, France. 1968

IN SEARCH OF GNONG by John Lahr. New York Free Press, N.Y.C. March 21, 1968

ONE SECOND PAST INFINITE by Nancy Hom. The Prattler. Brooklyn, New York. Feb. 13, 1968

"CRAZY SAM" AVITAL TEACHES SILENCE by John Neville. Dallas Morning News. Texas. Sept. 21, 1969

GRAN INTERPRETE DEL MIMO SAMUEL AVITAL ACTUARA EN 3 FUNCIONES El Imparcial. Guatemala. Nov. 22, 1969

MIMICO ISRAEL: ACTUARA HOY EN EL CONSERVATORIO La Hora. Equador. Nov. 22, 1969

EL GRAN "MIMO" SAMUEL AVITAL La Hora. Guatemala. Dec. 16, 1969

AVITAL IS MIME by Weaver P. Cleaver. Dallas News. Texas. Nov. 1970

GABBY VISITS THE UNDERGROUND FLICKS (Avital's film, "Pierrot visits New York") Dallas Notes. Texas. May 1970

AVITAL: MIME STUDENTS LEARN SELF-CONFRONTATION by Doug Stanglin. The Daily Campus SMU. Texas. Jan. 30, 1970

MIME SAMUEL AVITAL. MASTER OF THE SILENT ART SPEAKS by Scott Gibbs. Boulder, Colorado. Feb. 10, 1971

CHILDREN, ANIMALS, AND CLOWNS by Scott Gibbs. Boulder, Colorado. Oct. 5, 1971

PANTOMIMIC AVITAL THRILLS AUDIENCE Colorado Daily. Boulder, Colorado. Feb. 1, 1971

MIME MASTER SAYS WISE TO LISTEN TO
SILENCE The El Paso Times. April 6, 1971

SAM AVITAL'S SILENCE IS USUALLY
COMMUNICABLE by Carole McWilliams. Daily
Camera. Boulder, Colo. Sept. 5, 1971

MIME AVITAL—BREAKING DOWN BARRIERS
by Margie Dolph. Colorado Daily. Boulder,
Colorado. Sept. 14, 1971

AVITAL, ELFIN APOSTLE OF SILENCE by William
Gallo. Rocky Mountain News. Denver, Colorado.
Sept. 26, 1971

MIME WITH A MESSAGE by Will Schaleben.
Boulder Magazine. Boulder, Colorado. Dec. 2,
1971

AVITAL'S MIME REFLECTS TRAITS OF ALL by
William Gallo. Rocky Mountain News. Denver,
Colorado. Dec. 4, 1971

AVITAL REVEALS VALUE OF SILENCE by
William Gallo. Rocky Mountain News. Denver,
Colorado. Dec. 9, 1971

HOW DO YOU TALK TO A MIME? by Martha
Rost. Town and Country Review. Boulder,
Colorado. Dec. 21, 1971

MIME'S CLASS TO BE "LABORATORY OF THE
SELF" The Galveston Daily News. Galveston,
Texas. July 17, 1972

MIME MASKS AND MAKE-UP by Ann Bordelon.
Galveston Daily News. Galveston, Texas. July 30,
1972

LEAP THE LANGUAGE BARRIER Colorado Daily.
Boulder, Colorado. Sept. 11, 1972

NOISE CULPRIT FOR SILENT PANTOMIME by
Doug Smith. Courier Express. Buffalo, New York.
Sept. 1972

AVITAL HAS MUCH ON MIND ABOUT THE
ART OF MIME Courier Express. Buffalo, New
York. Sept. 17, 1972

MIME'S A DELIGHT IN COMIC SKETCHES by Jeff
Simon. Buffalo Evening News. New York. Sept.
30, 1972

SAMUEL AVITAL TALKS BY Samuel Maddox and
Bradford Morrow. Colorado Daily. Boulder,
Colorado. Nov. 17, 1972

THE ONE VIOLIN ORCHESTRA by Stephen
Foehr. Straight Creek Journal. Denver, Colorado.
Nov. 4, 1972

BOULDER MIME THEATER Straight Creek
Journal. Denver, Colorado. May 15, 1973

THE MIME OF SAMUEL AVITAL IS INDEED A
MAGICAL SILENCE by Barbralu Fried. Boulder
Daily Camera. Boulder, Colorado. Dec. 12, 1973

THE UNIQUE ART OF PANTOMIME by Samuel
Avital. The Rosicrucian Digest. San Jose,
California. Dec. 1973

MIME by Pauli Wanderer. Town and Country.
Boulder, Colorado. Dec. 12, 1973

AVITAL: MIME IS INTEGRATION OF ACTING
AND DANCE by Kenan S. Block. Colorado Daily.
Boulder, Colorado. Sept. 24, 1973

NEW BLOOD FOR THE ART OF MIME (Boulder
Mime Theater) by Carole McWilliams. Boulder
Daily Camera. Boulder, Colorado. June 30, 1974

PICTURES OF SILENCE by Barbralu Fried.
Boulder Daiy Camera. Boulder, Colorado. Jan.
20, 1974

SAMUEL AVITAL. ARTIST RATES SILENT
EXPRESSION by Richard Mial. La Crosse Tribune.
La Crosse, Wisconsin. July 29, 1974

WHAT ASTARIANS DO by Hildegarde Olsen.
Voice of Astara. Los Angeles, California. Aug.
1974

SAMUEL AVITAL: MIME'S THE WORD by Ben
Weaver. East West Journal. Boston, Mass. Sept.
1974

MIME: THE SPACE OF AN ART by Samuel Avital.
East West Journal. Feb. 1975

THE STATE OF MIME, interview with Samuel
Avital. Cake Eaters. Boulder, Colorado. March
1975

THE SPIRIT OF MIME by Samuel Avital. Psychic
Times. Berkeley, California. May 1975

Suggested Readings

THE THEATRE AND ITS DOUBLE by Antonin Artaud. Grove Press Inc. New York. 1958

TOWARDS A POOR THEATRE by Jersey Grotowsky. Clarion book. Simon and Schuster. New York. 1968

THE THINKING BODY by Mabel Elsworth Todd. Dance Horizons Inc. Brooklyn, New York. 1937

THE SUFIS by Idries Shah. Anchor Book. Doubleday and Co. Garden City, New York. 1966

THE EXPLOITS OF THE INCOMPARABLE MULLA NASRUDIN
THE MAGIC MONASTERY
WISDOM OF THE IDIOTS
THE DERMIS PROBE
by Idries Shah. Dutton Paperbacks. New York. 1971-72

CARAVAN OF DREAMS
THINKERS OF THE EAST
by Idries Shah. Penguin Books Inc. Baltimore, Maryland. 1972

ZEN FLESH, ZEN BONES by Paul Reps. Doubleday Anchor Book. Garden City, New York.

BE HERE NOW by Ram Das. Lama Foundation.

TONING by Laurel Elizabeth Keyes. DeVorss and Company. Santa Monica, California. 1973

9½ MYSTICS by Herbert Weiner. Collier Books. New York, 1969

THEATRE by Jacques Burdick. Newsweek Books. New York. 1974

MY AUTOBIOGRAPHY by Charles Chaplin. Simon and Schuster. New York. 1964

THE EMPTY SPACE by Peter Brook. Discus Books. Avon. The Hearst Corporation. 959 8th Ave. New York. 1968

THE TEACHINGS OF DON JUAN   1968
A SEPARATE REALITY   1971
JOURNEY TO IXTLAN   1972
TALES OF POWER   1974
by Carlos Casteneda. Simon and Schuster. New York. 10020

THE CIPHER OF GENESES   1967
THE SONG OF SONGS   1972
by Carlo Suares. Bantam. Shambhala. Berkeley, Calif.

THE CONFERENCE OF THE BIRDS by Farid-ud-Din Attar. Shambhala Publications. Berkeley, Calif. 1971

EL TOPO by Alexandro Jodorowsky. Douglas Book. The World Publishing Co. 1971

KABBALAH by Charles Ponce. Straight Arrow Books. San Francisco, Calif. 1973

THE MYSTIC SPIRAL by Jill Purce. Avon Books. The Hearst Corporation. New York. 1974

THE SETH MATERIAL
SETH SPEAKS
by Jane Roberts. Prentice Hall. Englewood Cliffs, New Jersey. 1970

THE SECOND BOOK OF DO-IN by Jacques De Langre. Happiness Press, Magalia, Calif. 1974

References and Bibliography

THE MIME by Jean Dorcy. Robert Speller and Sons, Publishers Inc. New York. 1961

THE HISTORY OF PANTOMIME by R.G. Broadbent. The Citadel Press. New York. 1964

BODY AND MIND IN HARMONY by Sophia Delza. David McKay Company Inc. New York. 1961

EYES ON MIME by Katherine Sorely Walker. The John Day Co. New York 1969

PANTOMIME * EXERCISES AND ELEMENTS by David Albert. University Press of Kansas. 1969

THE MIME BOOK by Claude Kipnis. Harper and Row, Publishers. New York. 1974

AWARENESS THROUGH MOVEMENT by Moshe Feldenkrais. Harper and Row, Publishers. New York. 1972

NOBODY AND MATURE BEHAVIOR by Moshe Feldenkrais. International Universities Press. New York. 1970

A LA RENCONTRE DE LA MIME by Jean Dorcy. Les Cahiers De Danse Et Culture. 4, Villa Roule a Nevilly-sur-Seine 1948

THE ART OF MIME by Irene Mawer. Expression Co. Publishers. Boston Mass, London. 1955

MIME THE TECHNIQUE OF SILENCE by Richmond Sheperd. Drama Book Specialists. New York. 1971

PANTOMIME, THE SILENT THEATRE by Douglas and Kari Hunt. Atheneum. New York. 1964

PAROLÈS SUR LE MIME by Etienne Decroux. Gallimad. Paris. 1963

EVERY LITTLE MOVEMENT by Ted Shawn. Dance Horizons Inc. Brooklyn, New York. 1954

NOUVELLE REFLECTIONS SUR LE THEATRE by J.L. Barrault. Flamarion. Paris. France. 1959

INITIATION AU MIME by Pierre Richy et J.C. de Mauraige. Paris. L'Amicale. 1960

THE ART OF PANTOMIME by Charles Aubert. Translated from the French by Edith Sears. Benjamin Bloom Inc. New York 1970

MIME JOURNAL NUMBER 1 Ed. by Thomas Leabhart Mime School Inc. Fayetteville, Arkansas. 1974

STANISLAVSKY ON THE ART OF THE STAGE. Translated by David Magarshack. Hill and Wang. New York. 1924

THE JEWISH CATALOGUE by Richard, Siegel, Michael Strassfeld, Sharon Strassfeld. The Jewish Publication Society of America. Philadelphia, Pennsylvania. 1973.

"...AVITAL.. The mime of a thousand faces and one..."

Michel Berger
Theatre critic, Paris, France.

"...His artistic personality, his natural talent and his obvious gift for Mime..."

Maximilien Decroux
Paris, France.

"...AVITAL has rediscovered some of the most marvelous charms of an art which will owe him much..."

Andre Veinstein, Author.
Theatre collections.
Bibliotheque de L'Arsenal
Paris, France.

"...In the wink of an eye he takes us from laughter to tears and at times both at once..."

Frances Duseberg
Comparaisons, Paris, France.

"...One undergoes an artistic experience seeing him. His electrifying appearance on stage establishes at once a unique and highly theatrical personality."

Moshe Hanahami
Poet, Writer, Theatre critic
Jerusalem, Israel.

"...His fantasy is startling, the irony sharp...Successful at condensing time and space in a gesture."

John Lahr
Village Voice, New York

" 'I am a graduate of the University of the streets of Paris!' says Avital. You know at once that his progress through such an unorthodox curriculum was not easy, demanding courage, resilience, and wit. But it is a course that produced a remarkably alive and loving artist, a fine example of the ancient art of silent theatre. AVITAL has come to the theatre department at S.M.U. spreading joyously the gospel of the expressive body."

Jack Clay
S.M.U. Theatre Dept.
Dallas, Texas.

"Samuel Avital is a lover of God-in-man. Many mystical schools teach that the real transmission takes place in and through the silence—through breath, heart, glance, and atmosphere. The danger lies when we make this a mere philosophy; the fulfillment comes when we make it a reality in our art, in our lives. I believe Samuel Avital's teachings are a real step in this direction."

Masheikh Wali Ali Meyer
San Francisco, California

"We are all, without exception, crazy

The saving grace of Avital's craziness is that it is concerned with his own spirituality. This concern has consumed every day of his life, and however myopic it may appear to some, it

is the matrix and meaning of Avital, the man and the artist."

Paul J. Curtis
Director
The American Mime Theatre
New York

"Somewhere in Colorado, in a beautiful town called Denver, there is a community of young people directed by the very talented Samuel Avital, I think that his work is important, he brings awareness to the soul of people, and gives to the young dedicated artists who work under his direction the need, dedication and love for the world of silence, the beautiful Art of Pantomime."

Marcel Marceau, BIP

"If you seek some truth or direction in life or art, stay close to Samuel for he might just then crawl out of his shell and give you of his soul."

Moni Yakim
Director Pantomime Theatre
of New York.

"It has been a tradition in Mime since the turn of the century to present ones work in a complete and classical manner. Every gesture has its precise meaning; every piece calls to mind a tribute to Aristotle. For example, one might see Marceau over a period of years and always see essentially the same performance. And while there is beauty to this classical approach which is undeniably breathtaking in its technique, it often borders on extremely fragile stylism. It is as if we were watching a ballerina in a music box.

AVITAL'S Mime shatters this tradition with the bright splash of a belly laugh. He establishes in his work an immediacy of communication that recalls the roots of Mime in tribal ceremony. His most refined tool unquestionably is his improvisational technique. It is remarkably sharp and supple, and each of his performances is truly unique for it.

Using his pieces as frameworks, he builds in a comic, poignant manner characters that blow up to giants or diminish to insects, then pushes them out to the brink of disaster. Avital always threatens to be excessive, yet he always seems to rescue himself (and us) in the nick of time.

Indeed it is that breathless improvisational quality of his work that excites us; We are caught suspended with Avital on a high wire, and in that bright timelessness we realize the real beauty of theatre. For Avital is drawing his inspiration not only from the grand tradition, but from his audience, from "THE NOW". Through the earthy humor of a juggler, Avital creates a moment of holy silence. It is that paradoxical marriage of the sacred and the profane, of art and spirit, that is his trademark and his genius."

Michel de la Flame

"The silence is dynamique...
Everything that is produced in time is dynamique...
The movement is dynamique...
The silence is dynamique...
Avital could not choose a better name for his center than the center of silence.

Moshe Naim

BIOGRAPHY

Born in Morocco of Jewish Kabbalists, AVITAL's life has been a "CARAVAN OF DREAMS". He has studied farming, Physics and religion in Israel, played to crowds, in Guatemala and Sweden, and taught in the streets of Manhattan and in the mountains of Colorado.

At 14, Avital travelled alone to Israel where he spent 10 years and also was in a Kibbutz in Gallilee. A chance night spent watching Chaplin's Limelight gave him the inner inspiration to go to Paris and learn the silent art of Mime.

He began with Dance and Drama at the Sorbonne, but soon found himself under the world's Master Teacher of Mime, Etienne Decroux. Many years of study, often "sitting on a bench, tired, sad and very hungry," gave AVITAL the beautiful, warm sense of humor and improvisational sharpness that are his trademarks.

AVITAL spent the 60's travelling and performing all over the world. He has toured extensively appearing with the troup of Maximilien Decroux in Europe, performing as a solo-mime in Amsterdam and Stockholm and playing throughout North and South America—in cafes, theatres, films and television.

For the past several years, AVITAL has conducted Mime workspaces at Southern Methodist University,New York City and, recently, in Boulder, Colorado where he now lives.

For this man that was called "the gradute of the University of the streets of Paris" and "the Mime of a thousand faces and one", Mime has become a way of life. Mime for him is grasping the void.